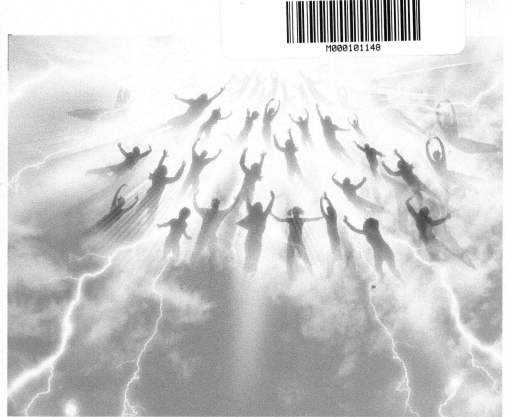

IN THE TWINKLING OF AN EYE

MY TRUE EXPERIENCE:

I WAS RAPTURED AND RECEIVED A NEW GLORIFIED BODY

JESUS HELD ME IN HIS ARMS AND I LOOKED INTO THE EYES OF GOD

by Tony Lamb

See my new web site, with tons of FREE stuff at: www.tonylamb.org

‖

Forward

Does anyone alive truly know what it feels like to be in the arms of God, to feel his arms around you, to look into His eyes?

I do because I was Raptured and this was so much more than 'just a dream'.

This was one dream that I wish I had never woken up from.

Because I was going 'HOME' .
This was no mere 'dream', this was earth shattering and eye opening and after this 'dream' I knew I would never be the same.

I was safe, secure and loved by the creator and safe in his loving arms.

What a mighty and awesome God we serve.

My God is the one and only true living God.

My God is the God of Abraham.

The God of Isaac.

The God of Jacob.

The God of Moses.

And the God of my Mother.

My God is that God.

My God spoke the Universe into existence.

My God made all things, for NOTHING exists that my God did not make.

My God stands alone without equal and without peer.

My God can do anything, all things except lie or fail.

My God is the Alpha and the Omega,

Without beginning and without end.

My God is from everlasting to everlasting,

My God always was and will always be 'God'.

My God has unlimited power.

My God knows all things because he made all things,

Everything seen and unseen, everything known and unknown,

My God made it all.

My God knows the number of hairs upon your head.

My God knows what you do in the dark behind closed doors.

My God is the ultimate creator and the ultimate judge of all things.

And one day my God will judge you and me.

One day every knee will bow and every tongue shall confess that my God, IS GOD.

John 1
1. In the beginning was the word, and the word was with God and the word was God.

2. The same was in the beginning with God.

3. All things were made by him; and without him was not anything made that was made.

4. In him was life; and the life was the light of men.

5. And the light shineth in darkness; and the darkness comprehended it not.

14. And the word was made flesh, and dwelt among us, (and we beheld his glory, the glory as of the only begotton of the Father), full of grace and truth.

Several months ago, the Lord led me to write this book.

I was told to share what the Holy Spirit gave me.

I give All Praise, All Glory and All Honor to God.

I seek nothing for myself. Everything I make from my books I donate.

One night at 3 AM I was startled with a very loud, hard and heavy KNOCK, KNOCK, KNOCK on my bedroom door. I was shocked and I called out to my wife but she didn't answer me, as she was sound asleep.

I just wrote it off as a twilight kind of dream.   BUT two nights later and again at 3 AM
I heard a very loud and hard KNOCK, KNOCK, KNOCK on my bedroom door.

Funny thing is both nights I was having trouble getting to sleep, so I was awake but, I was trying to get to sleep.

Have you EVER heard of anyone having a dream where someone was knocking loudly on his (or her) bedroom door and having the exact same dream twice, one day apart?

But this second time I answered the knock on my bedroom door.
I spoke up loudly and I said:

'YES LORD I AM AWAKE'.

Another time I was sleeping and someone spoke to me and said:
'Wake Up And Tell The People'.   And then I heard a bell ringing.

Now this bell that I heard was like an old fashion alarm clock with the two bells on top and the little hammer (or striker) would go back and forth between the bells.   It makes a very distinctive sound.

And even today when you think of an alarm clock you think of this type of old-fashioned alarm clock.   Anyway, that was the type of bell I heard ringing.

A few moments later, again and even louder I heard a voice say:
'WAKE UP AND TELL THE PEOPLE'.   And again, I heard the same bell ringing.

Then a third time the voice was very stern, almost yelling at me to:
'WAKE UP AND TELL THE PEOPLE'.

And just like before I heard a bell ringing, but this time I woke up and realized my phone was ringing on my nightstand.

I got the message Lord, NOW I AM AWAKE, AND NOW I AM TELLING THE PEOPLE...

Our time is short and as the world grows dark, we must let our light shine all the brighter,

FOR THE KING IS COMING (and soon).

In these dark days we are NOT to hide our light under a bushel basket. (But Lord you gave me a 'Flame Thrower' how I can hide this).

I was called as a Watchman with dreams and visions.
I am just the Dust of the Earth - But I am God's Dirt.

I am not a Minister, Deacon or even a Sunday school teacher.
But I am born again and washed in the blood of Jesus.

I am a Watchman on the Wall with dreams and visions, watching for the soon return of Jesus Christ.

I was called to be a Watchman.
My authority comes from Ezekiel 33: 1 through 9 (with an emphasis on verse 6)

I cannot speak for other Watchmen. (I just know God called me to do this.)

Starting in 2014 I started having Tribulation dreams and some were very disturbing.

Then in early 2015 God gave me what I would call: was a very hard calling.

I describe my hard calling in my book titled: 'GOD SHOWED ME THE FUTURE, America Is Entering Judgement' by Tony Lamb.

I have had a multitude of conformations to speak about my dreams.

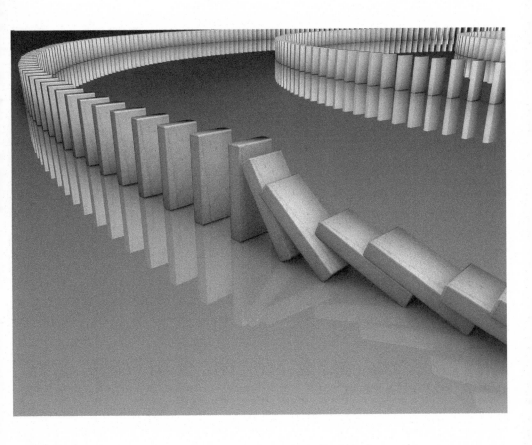

DEUTERONOMY 19:15
AT THE MOUTH OF TWO WITNESSES OR AT THE MOUTH OF
THREE WITNESSES SHALL A MATTER BE ESTABLISHED.

People who I love and trust have told me to speak.

People would be talking to me and in their conversation, they would say:

'It's time to Speak'.

The Holy Spirit gave me dreams where a voice told me: **'BE NOT AFRAID, SPEAK'**

The Holy Spirit gave me dreams where I was told: **'IT'S TIME TO SPEAK'**.

The Holy Spirit also told me: **'THIS IS YOUR CALLING'**.

One night the Holy Spirit gave me this message:
'IF YOU DO NOT HAVE THE COURAGE TO SPEAK NOW, THEN YOU WILL NOT HAVE THE COURAGE TO (NOT DENY ME LATER').

One night this scripture was shown to me at random by the Holy Spirit:

ACTS 18:9
THEN SPOKE THE LORD TO PAUL BY A NIGHT VISION, SPEAK HOLD NOT THY PEACE.

My Sunday school teacher Brother Danny looked right at me and as part of his lesson said: **'BE NOT AFRAID SPEAK'**   (Not Once, BUT TWICE IN THE SAME LESSON).

Then I went home and read a note on my nightstand that I had written to myself from Holy Spirit the night before. The Holy Spirit had woke me up at 1 AM and gave me a message, so I wrote it down, but being sleepy I quickly went back to sleep and I forgot about the note.

But when I got home from Sunday church, I was reminded that I had written a note to myself the night before.
I opened the note and I was shocked to read: - **'BE NOT AFRAID SPEAK'**.

God is Amazing and He never ceases to surprise me and inspire me.

The Holy Spirit told me I had a connection with Moses as he was not a public speaker either (Moses had a stutter, so: 'I WAS IN GOOD COMPANY'.)

The Holy Spirit showed me I had a connection with Jonah as he also told God 'NO' and like me he ran from God, but it didn't work for Jonah, and it didn't work for me either.

The Holy Spirit also showed me I had a connection with Noah, as he also had only one message that he preached for over 100 years. Noah preached to repent and to enter the door of the Ark for Salvation from what was to come upon the Earth.

But no one came and no one listened and no one repented.
And no one entered the Ark except for Noah and his family.

Like Noah, I also have just one message, and that message is:

Time is short, repent and trust in Jesus for Salvation as He is the door of the Ark by which all must enter for Salvation from what is also to come shortly upon the earth.

And there be few who listen and few who heed the warning.

(By myself I am not a public speaker).

BUT
I
AM
WHO
'YOU'
SAY
I
AM
LORD

I will trust in God and walk by faith, not by sight.

Who am I to doubt or question God?

Being a servant of Almighty God who tells me to 'SPEAK' I am offering to speak at your church (or about any other venue) FREE without any fee.

I do this (NOT) for my glory but to glorify the one who sent me, Jesus Christ who I give All Praise, All Glory and All Honor to Forever and Ever.

God commands me to speak – SO I WILL SPEAK.

My topics include but are not limited to:
My Calling, Prophecy, What is Coming, What God Showed Me, the Time of Sorrows, the Tribulation, The Rapture of the Faithful, Why so Few People Feel or Hear From God and Putting God First.

I am NOT a Minister or a Prophet. Though I talk a lot about prophecy that is due to the fact that I am a Watchman who has been given Dreams and Visions by the Holy Spirit.

Most of these dreams and visions were about the Time of Sorrows and the Tribulation.

But one dream was a Rapture dream and that dream was so unbelievable that I wrote a whole book about my Rapture dream I call it: '**IN THE TWINKLING OF AN EYE – My True Experience: I was Raptured And Received A New Glorified Body**'.

This dream was the most intense and vivid dream I have ever had and it was one dream I wish I had not woken up from. This dream was full of emotion and I felt love like I have never felt before. This dream was Joy Unspeakable.

SO, I am not a prophet but my dreams give me insight into the future. And God told me to share it with you. So that is why I offer to speak to your congregation.

In a nutshell our time is critically short. Are you watching the news?

The Holy Spirit gave me this Warning:

'NOW, It's Like Watching The Clock Tick Down To An Execution'.
For we all have sinned and fallen short in the eyes of God, and if it were
not for the blood of Jesus we ALL would have a date with the
executioner.

THANK YOU JESUS!

THESE ARE SOME OF THE WAYS THE HOLY SPIRIT HAS SPOKE TO
ME

1. The Holy Spirit speaks to me in a still quiet voice in my head or my heart
or both.

2. I recognize that quiet voice as the Holy Spirit, as I have heard it many
times.

3. The Holy Spirit gives me Dreams

4. The Holy Spirit gives me Visions

5. The Holy Spirit physically touches me, and has sent a mild electric shock
throughout my whole body.

6. And the Holy Spirit has physically shaken my whole body while lying in
bed.

7. By speaking in tongues.

8. By my shaking in the spirit.

9. The Holy Spirit has floated above me in bed and spoke to me many times, I don't know if this is a dream or a vision because I do not open my eyes, but I feel like I am awake.

10. The physical manifestation (by moving things in my room) while I was awake and, in the room, but my back was turned. (This is very rare and only happened once).

I prayed hard over this and after 3 days of praying the Holy Spirit then confirmed it was Him that moved the object and why.

And amazingly the Holy Spirit has found other ways to speak to me. Again, God never ceases to amaze me and surprise me.

 These Are The Last Days.

The Holy Spirit has put this in my heart.

Acts 2:17
And it shall come to pass in the last days saith God, I will pour out my Spirit upon all flesh: and your sons and your daughters shall prophesy, and your young men shall see visions, and your old men shall dream dreams.

I have seen an outpouring of the Holy Spirit in my church like I have never seen before.

Funny thing is we went to church AND GOD SHOWED UP… 'In a big way'. The Preacher never even got to preach his message as the Holy Spirit took control of the service and made it HIS service. NOW that is the kind of church I am talking about.

God Bless you, God Keep you, and God make his face shine upon you and give you peace.

(I am just the dust of the earth, but I am God's dirt)

Watchman Tony Lamb

[]   []

You can find this book and all my books at: www.tonylamb.org

THANK YOU JESUS
You can email me or write to me at the address listed here.

NOW

IT'S LIKE WATCHING

THE CLOCK TICK DOWN

TO AN EXECUTION

 **Introduction**

My name is Tony Lamb

It seems like everyone is having Rapture dreams these days.

Youtube is covered up with Rapture dreams, 4-year-old s are having Rapture dreams.   98-year-old s are having Rapture dreams, everyone is having Rapture dreams.

BUT when you get into these videos of these Rapture dreams most of these people are having vague and highly subjective Rapture dreams.

NOW I AM NOT saying you cannot have a vague Rapture dream and the Holy Spirit confirm it, give you scriptures to go with it. Remember, at the mouth of two or three witnesses shall a matter be established.

NOW that said just because someone has a dream where they see a field of 7 cows and they turn away but when they look back, they only see 3 cows.

At least with this type of Rapture dream you have someone (in this case cows) that are missing.   Without more input from the Holy Spirit, I would just call this a missing cow dream.

BUT some of these so-called Rapture dreams are so farfetched, nothing and no one goes missing, there is no input (or confirmation) from the Holy Spirit then these ODD dreams may be chalked up to bad pizza rather than being a Rapture dream.

I never had much interest in Rapture dreams until I had my Rapture dream and then I became very interested and only then did I realize the gamut of Rapture dreams that were out there.

My wife and I started attending a small rural First Assembly of God Church in Western Arkansas in 2013.

My first thought on this was I was only doing this because my wife wanted me to go to church with her.   My wife was invited to church, by a good friend of hers from work.   And after about a year of her friend asking my wife decided to go to church, so we ended up going.

I thought I could pitch in a little change in the offering plate and sit there inconspicuous, but God saw me sitting there and started dealing with me. And soon repented and I started praying and seeking the Lord in earnest.

I asked the Lord for a work I could do for my church. I have a bad left knee from arthritis pain and have trouble walking or standing very long.

I saw others mowing the church lawn or vacuuming and cleaning the church so I prayed for the Lord to give me a work that I could do for my church.

Our minister told us of a prayer, where he asked the Lord to shape and mold him like the clay on the potter's wheel. Into anything, any shape that was pleasing to the Lord. And to fill his cup to overflowing with his spirit.

I thought that was a GREAT prayer, so I prayed that prayer. LET ME TELL YOU GOD SHOWED UP AND ANSWERED MY PRAYER IN A MIGHTY AND COMPELLING WAY.

Sometimes when you pray you get much more than what you ask for.

We are sometimes reminded to NOT hide our light under a bushel basket, but to let our light shine for the Lord.

It seems that most Christians get a little penlight.
BUT LORD YOU GAVE ME A FLAME THROWER

I am reminded in so many ways to speak.

The Bible will tell me to speak.

My dreams tell me to speak.

The Sunday school teacher tells me to speak.

The Holy Spirit tells me to speak.

I am commanded by the Holy Spirit to '**Wake Up And Tell The People**'

Acts 18:9 Then spoke the Lord to Paul by a night vision, Speak Hold Not Thy Peace.

The Holy Spirit asked me to speak to my church congregation.

The Holy Spirit has asked me to speak to people.

The Holy Spirit asked me to go door to door and pass out church fliers.

The Holy Spirit asked me to display a sign out on a city street in front of Walmart

The Holy Spirit asked me to start a new Christian web site which I did at www.tonylamb.org

The Holy Spirit asked me to talk on the radio

The Holy Spirit asked me to give

The Holy Spirit asked me to testify

The Holy Spirit asked me to write books

The Holy Spirit asked me to pass out free Bibles

The Holy Spirit asked me to make youtube videos.

The Holy Spirit asked me to start a youtube ministry, you can go to
www.youtube.com and in the search box type in my name [Tony Lamb]
and it should take you to my youtube page where you can see all my videos.
I never asked WHY, or said later or maybe or no. I am very happy to be a
humble servant of the most high and almighty God.

None of this I do for my glory but to glorify the one who sent me.

**Romans 14:11 For it is written, As I live, saith the Lord, every knee shall
bow to me and every tongue shall confess to God.**

I am just the dust of the earth,

I am nothing, I am nobody

BUT I am God's dirt.

I am not a Minister, Deacon or even a Sunday School teacher.
But I have been called to be a Watchman with dreams and visions.

I am NOT a prophet but my dreams and visions of the Time of Sorrows, The Tribulation and the Rapture gives me insight into end times events.

1 Corinthians 13: 9 For we know in part, and we prophesy in part.

1 Corinthians 13:12 For now we see through a glass, darkly

1 Corinthians 14:4 He that speaketh in an unknown tongue edifieth himself; but he that prophesieth edifieth the church

The Holy Spirit prompted me to write this book. The Holy Spirit came to me over and over giving me little bits and pieces of information about Heaven.

I guess this was so I would have the time to write this down before going on to more information. Now I sleep with pen and paper on my nightstand just in case the Holy Spirit gives me more information that way I can quickly write it down.

I understand that most information about Heaven is supposed to be secret except for a few details.

So, the question is why me Lord and why now am I getting all this information about Heaven?

What the Holy Spirit revealed to me was that since the Rapture is so close that Jesus wants you to know what will be your reward (to a point).

As many parts are still a big secret, the Holy Spirit will not reveal anything that I am not to know or share.   The Holy Spirit tells me that there is a lot more that is kept hidden about Heaven then what is revealed, so with that said you will be surprised even shocked at the majesty and grandeur of it all.

I know this phrase has been used a lot but here it fits more than any place else.

Words cannot tell, eyes have not seen and ears have not heard the majesty and the beauty you will behold in Heaven.

Everyone has the idea that in heaven you will be sitting on a cloud and playing a harp for ever and ever.

But nothing could be farther from the truth.   NOW if that is what you want, I guess it could be arranged for you.

But for most people that would be a very boring existence.   And that is exactly what Satan wants you to think and many people think that is what heaven is all about.

But the truth is heaven is perfect for everyone.   If you love the beach and palm trees that is what you will see in your corner of heaven.

If you love a desert climate and that is your idea of heaven that is where you will be.   Everyone gets their own piece of heaven.

I cannot guarantee this, this is what I feel in my spirit, as if the Holy Spirit revealed it to me.   I do not know how to explain it any better. I just 'feel' it to be so.

The Holy Spirit has already given me so very much. I pray the Holy Spirit brings it all back to my memory so I can get it all on paper. That is my prayer.

All Praise, All Glory, All Honor to God who sits on the throne most high above all.   Jesus is the way, the truth and the life.

Chapter 1
MY RAPTURE DREAM

For several years I had been given end of days and Tribulation dreams and visions some of these dreams were disturbing to say the least.

I did not pray for a Rapture dream the Holy Spirit just gave it to me. (Thank You Holy Spirit.)

My dream (the condensed version):
I was standing in a field of grass, on a knoll and it was night but I saw lights from houses off in the not too far distant, there was moon light and the stars were out.

For some reason I did not think this strange or out of place, I was just there standing in the middle of this field looking up.

Then without any warning there was an instant shaft of brilliant light that enveloped me. I could not see outside this shaft of brilliant light and it was an extremely bright white light.

Then all of a sudden, I found myself outside the shaft of light and I was about 20 feet away from the shaft of white light. The light seemed to be as bright as the sun but it didn't hurt your eyes to look at it.

It was like looking at a lightning bolt only much bigger.   I was staring at the shaft of light when I realized there were other shafts of light that were developing and enveloping other people around me some were just yards away while others were ¼ mile and still some were miles away.

I was made aware that my Rapture experience was slowed down for me. While I was watching others being enveloped by the shaft of light it was almost instantaneous for others. I saw these shafts of light travel straight down to the earth and envelope people and just as quick they traveled back up to Heaven.

Some people have a saying about being fast as lightening, BUT when you are watching a storm you can actually see lightening travel down to the ground. This light was so fast if you blinked you could miss the whole event; it was just that fast.

From my vantage point I guess maybe I saw about 1000 (more or less) shafts of light hit the ground envelope people and just as fast they were ascending back from where they came. All I can tell you is that there were a lot of shafts of light and too many to count, so my estimate could be higher or lower.

Keep in mind that I did not have time to turn and look behind me, I just knew that the shafts of light were behind me as well. And these shafts if light were taking people with it as they streaked up and out of sight.

This whole process, the light coming down and enveloping people and then streaking back up took only a fraction of a second. Literally if you blinked just at the right time you could miss the whole event.

And in that event what you would see is a person standing, then you blink your eyes and then you would notice they were simply gone.

The streak of light trailing these shafts of light seemed to be more of a (tracer effect) at least that was my observation and thoughts on this. But this tracer effect was not a long drawn out thing, as it also was very quick and it did not trail very far behind the light as it traveled down or up.

These shafts of light did not spend any time on the ground as it was an instant event coming down to earth and just as quick they ascended up and out of sight in an instant.

Then I was back inside my shaft of light and what I saw made my heart sink. I saw Jesus above me but he was slowly ascending, and NOT coming down to me. I lifted up my arms and I cried out begging, pleading, almost crying:

'Jesus Please, PLEASE Don't Leave Me'.

When I said that Jesus slowly came down to me and put his arms around me.

YES LORD

I AM AWAKE

Now I know at this point some people would ask:
'Did Jesus feet touch the ground?'

I was NOT looking at his feet, but as for my feet I didn't feel any ground under my feet.

So I would have to say NO Jesus feet did not touch the ground.

The instant Jesus wrapped his arms around me I was transformed. I was in a new body, I was young again, I felt no pain or suffering. I felt a warmth and genuine love and compassion that was totally indescribable. I felt a peace, love and compassion that was true and genuinely indescribably.

Another thing that I was impressed with was the fact that every single care, concern or worry melted away into nothing. I felt like; if I were dying of cancer, that worry would melt into nothing.

As NOTHING of this world mattered any longer. If your house was being foreclosed on, your car being repossessed, if your wife was in jail for drugs and you kids worked at a meth lab all that no longer mattered.

As every care of this world simple melted away into forgetfulness.

Even if you were lying on a hospital bed dying of cancer, nothing of this earth mattered in that place.

People who do drugs talk about the perfect high, where you forget everything and you forget your troubles. This was a million times better than the most perfect high ever described or imagined.

I felt a peace and a love that was absolutely indescribable. There is an old hymn called 'Joy Unspeakable' That is what I felt JOY UNSPEAKABLE and Full of Glory.

I felt Peace, Joy, Love, indescribable love, unfathomable love, a love without end, pure love, love eternal, boundless love, a love without condition, a love beyond expression or understanding and beyond comprehension.

So, my tiny 3-pound brain cannot fathom the boundless love God has for us. And the rewards he will lavish upon us, his children. The love I described is the love God has for all of us, if only we will turn from our sinful ways and seek his face and pray to be in God's will and grace.

Hell was not made for people but for demons and fallen angels but when we rebel against God and turn away from him. Then Hell will be full of people who refuse to seek God, who refuse to heed his warnings and be in God's will and grace.

There is a Heaven and yes there is a Hell and everyone goes to one place or the other. And if you think by NOT making a choice you can get out of this, by not making a choice (is a choice to not follow Jesus).

Chapter 2
IN THE WILL AND GRACE

It's not a single church or a religion that will get you to Heaven. It is your heart, your faith and your obedience to God that will get you to Heaven. Almost every time I pray, I pray to be pleasing to God, for if I am not pleasing to God then all is lost.

And it's more than just getting on my knees and sincerely praying also. You must be attentive and obedient to God. When God (more correctly the Holy Spirit) puts it in your heart to give someone a couple dollars or knock on a door and ask them if they know the saving grace of Jesus Christ and invite them to church, (do you do it?)

Has God ever asked you to go door-to-door and ask people if they know of the love of Jesus? Right there is where you will lose about 90% of the people in your church.

(That is why these Christian churches are not going door-to-door and knocking on doors)?

You need to be attentive and obedient to God when he tugs at your heart strings to do a thing, (you need to do it).

The Holy Spirit once asked me to go door-to-door and pass out church fliers. But my church had no literature so I had to make up my own fliers on my computer.

Now with that said the Holy Spirit knows I have a bad left knee so He only asked me to pass out 5 fliers. I didn't say NO, or I can't do it, I just made up the fliers and I got my cane and I hobbled from door to door passing out my fliers, and inviting people to church.

Once the Holy Spirit asked me to make up a poster and display it out on the city street in front of Walmart.   I made up my sign but then the Holy Spirit told me 'NO that is not what I want you to say'.   The Holy Spirit gave me a message for my poster and that message was: 'SUDDEN DESTRUCTION COMES – DO YOU KNOW JESUS'.

The Holy Spirit then asked me on three different occasions to sit out in front of Walmart on the city street and display my sign beside a homeless man and his dog. I didn't say, NO or I can't do that, or maybe - or someday.
I did it because the Holy Spirit asked me to do it.

We are supposed to walk by faith not by sight. I do not tell you this to brag as I am nothing, nobody, I am just the dust of the earth, BUT I am God's dirt.

Am I perfect?   Absolutely not, I stumble and fall often. I have made more mistakes then most Christians.

And I talk about being attentive and obedient, I several times knew it was the Holy Spirit asking me to do something and I don't know why but I didn't do it. (Now this said this is not something I am proud of, but I just want you to know that we all make mistakes, we all stumble and fall).

BUT when I stumble, when I am not obedient to God, I know where to go to get forgiveness.   I get on my knees and I have a very long humble and sincere talk with the Lord and I repent very hard for my failings. My God is all powerful, who knows all things and thankfully he is a loving kind Father who loves us so much and he is quick to forgive and slow to anger.

With that said: I hear some Christians say it's a small sin, it's only a little lie and I will repent for it later.

Some Christians say: Once Saved Always Saved.
No, you can back-slide, you can fall into sin and in that case, you need to humble yourself before Almighty God and repent of your sins in Jesus name.

I repent of my sins daily, just in case I have a little sin that creeps in unaware. I do not want to take a chance, so I repent every time I pray.

Some people believe everyone goes to heaven; I am afraid that is also a lie.

Some people do not believe in a Pre-Tribulation Rapture. They believe in a Mid-Tribulation or Post-Tribulation Rapture. The problem here is that a Post-Tribulation Rapture is NOT scriptural. And you must ask yourself just why do these Post-Tribers attack violently the Pre-Tribers. Satan at work again. Satan knows that IF he can get you to doubt and then believe the Post-Trib. Lie then he knows he has you.

After all who could stand under threat of having your head chopped off? And even if you could stand strong with that threat Satan knows full well you will cave in and take the Mark of the Beast when your wife, mother, father, children are tortured and threatened with death before your very eyes. He knows if he can get you to doubt the Pre-Tribulation Rapture then he will get you in the Tribulation and then he will have you (almost ALL OF YOU).

[]

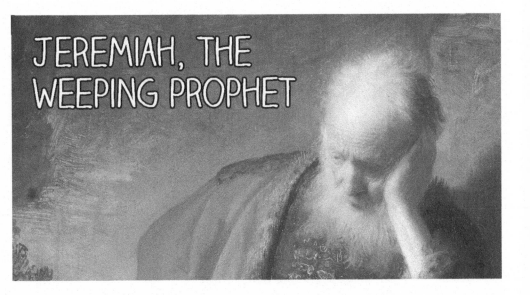

Jeremiah wept over what was lost.

That is NOT a very good attitude for a Christian to have. Remember God knows your heart. And if it's your attitude that you will sin now and repent later for it, what do you think God thinks about that?

Just maybe because you kneel down and mouth the words if you have it in your heart that in a similar situation you will do the same again, thinking you will just repent AGAIN. What do you think God thinks about that? Maybe God will not be so fast to forgive your sin the next time.

Our time on this earth is but a mist and vapor and it's gone. NOTHING of this earth is MORE important than where your soul will spend eternity, NOTHING.   We are just traveling through this place to get to our REAL permanent home in HEAVEN.

I don't know why God showed me so many dreams and visions. I did pray on several occasions that God mold me as the clay on the potter's wheel into anything that was pleasing to him. And then I would ask that he would fill my cup to overflowing with his spirit.

When my dreams started, I would cry. I would cry so hard like when you lose a precious loved one.   Tears would gush down my face, down my chest and even flowing into my lap.   Then I cried a lot and often, sometimes my wife would walk in on me and ask;

'Why are you crying'?
And through my sobbing I would tell her: 'A Lot of People Are Going to Get Hurt'
or 'I know What Is Coming'.

1 Corinthians 13: 9 For we know in part, and we prophesy in part.

1 Corinthians 13: 12 For now we see through a glass darkly

And no I don't know everything, I have only seen little bits and pieces of the future. But what I saw terrifies me and I am so thankful for the saving grace of Jesus Christ.

Because what is coming for sinners after the Rapture is truly horrific. No words can do what is coming justice. Murder, rape, all manner of vile acts that man can do to fellow man.

There will be demons released upon the earth and they will possess many people making them do unspeakable horrors.

Then the Nephilim will return to walk the earth again and their carnage will be indescribable.

But the most violent and dangerous will be the Fallen Angels who will walk the earth for their season of destruction.

The Bible says:
Revelation 9: 14 & 15
Saying to the sixth angel which had the trumpet, loose the four angels which are bound in the great river Euphrates.

And the four angels were loosed, which were prepared for an hour, and a day, and a month, and a year for to slay the third part of men.

DO YOU
KNOW
WHAT
TIME
IT IS

Then there will be all manner of diseases, pestilence, famine, earthquakes, volcanoes, asteroid strikes, the sun will turn dark, the moon will turn blood red, the earth will reel to and FRO like a drunkard, men, beasts and crops will be scorched with heat.

For several years I have kept my mouth shut about cannibalism, thinking it was maybe too graphic for some people. But a little over a year ago the Lord told me to tell it all, so I am telling you I have had several dreams where cannibalism was being practiced.

I was shown that one day the act of cannibalism would become accepted as normal and expected. This will take hold in a big way when the food runs out, then people will turn to eating pets, then rats and then bark, leaves, grass, bugs and worms.

And finally, they will eat each other as that will be all there is to eat. Now you know why the wealthy are buying and installing and stocking underground bunkers. They know what is coming.

Luke 21: 11
And great earthquakes shall be in divers places, and famines and pestilence's; and fearful sights and great signs shall there be from heaven.

Now you may think I read this verse and then had my dreams of the Tribulation, but it's the other way around. I first had the dreams and then I was shown this verse and others.

The point is a lot of people pray and call themselves Christians, but how many of them really follow the KJV Bible?

How many of them are obedient to the Holy Spirit?

How many of them put God second, third or even last?

God demands the first fruits as an offering or the perfect unblemished lamb as a sacrifice.

God expects, demands and deserves to be first, the head and never the tail. After all, look what Jesus did for you? He died on a cross for your sins and his death and his blood opened a way for our salvation.

So, God deserves the best, the first and instead of tithing 10% how about 11% how about giving in the offering plate when it's passed around. How about buying Bibles to be given out free at your church for visitors.

So, if your question is why doesn't God hear my prayers maybe you should re-read the above paragraph and ask yourself are you pleasing to God.

Are you putting God first? God will not accept or bless an offering that is second, or blemished or not of the first fruits or not your fair share.

I do not know why God gave me my Rapture Dream, but I am oh so thankful He did.

Chapter 3
THE LIGHT

In my dream I saw a powerful and ultra-bright white light envelope me while I was standing in a field. Do you know about the anti-aircraft flood lights of World War II? It was like that except it was shining down from above and it was like an instant on and off. Looking at this light seemed to be like looking at the sun but it didn't hurt your eyes.

While I was inside this light, I could see nothing outside the light. But then I was instantly placed outside the tube of brilliant bright light for a moment of time. I could not tell you how long I was outside the shaft of light as the whole process was slowed down for me, but it seemed like it was just mere seconds.

But what I saw outside the shaft of light was amazing. What I saw were other shafts of light that were flashing down and then back up so fast that if you blinked just right you would miss the whole thing.

I was also amazed at how my Rapture was in super, super slow motion but everyone else that had been Raptured it was in real time. I was thinking: 'how is this possible'?

(No not everyone got Raptured) I saw a lot of people standing and looking in amazement and astonishment at this unreal event but they were not Raptured, they were not enveloped by these beams of white light. They were left behind.

I saw shafts of light exploding into view to my right, to my left, in front and behind me. Some were yards away while others seemed to be quite a ways from me. Some were ¼ mile or a ½ mile away and many others seemed to be miles from me.

For only a split second I saw what looked like a thousand of shafts of light everywhere all around me. But one thing is, the shafts of light seemed to be instantaneous, here, then gone.

There seemed to be a slight tracer effect of the light as it streaked up higher and higher and then out of sight.   This was simply an amazing sight and I have never seen anything like it ever. Almost like a tracer from a bullet being fired from a gun. But this effect was not a long drawn out affair as it was also quick and very short.

I don't think anyone has ever seen anything like this?
And it was not one here than one there, this ALL happened at the very same instant.

It all took less than a single blink of the eyes and the whole event was over. It was all over in less than of a second 1/10th of a second or 1/50th of a second how do you measure time that is that fast.

All I do know is that IF you blinked just right you could miss the whole event.   My God is an amazing God, limitless power, limitless love and all he asks from us is worship and that we love him like He loves us.

There are many references to light in the Bible.   The light that shown from Moses face, when he came down the mountain after talking to God. His face shone so bright they had to put a veil over his face because the glory of God shown so brightly on his face that it frightened the people. That is the kind of bright I am talking about.

The Glory of God will be shown round about you at that time.
And God will cause his very face to shine upon you and give you peace.
That is what I am praying for and watching for, that blessed hope.

There were many people that were left behind, some were crying uncontrollably, some had a 'deer caught in the headlights look'.   A kind of like: 'What Just Happened Look'.

Chapter 4
JESUS CAME DOWN TO ME FROM ABOVE

While I was outside the shaft of brilliant white light it was an almost instant event and I found myself back inside the shaft of light.

I looked up and I saw Jesus but he was slowly going up and not down to me so I cried out:

'Jesus Please, PLEASE Don't Leave Me'

I did this as if I was begging, pleading almost crying for Jesus not to leave me.

Jesus was wearing a very brilliant white robe that shone like the sun with a sash around his waist and he was wearing sandals upon his feet. He had long brown wavy hair and a full beard. (That was what I saw)

Jesus slowly came down to me.   It seemed highly symbolic to me but I failed to grasp the meaning of it.   (that is; Jesus coming down to me) Again my little 3-pound brain is too small to grasp the meaning of it, so I will have to leave it on faith and believe.

I know some people would ask: 'Did you see the nail holes in his hands or His feet?'

To be honest I was so excited with what was happening I did not think to look for nail holes.

My personal feeling was at this point, He didn't need to prove who he was.

(This I will take on faith - I will tell you this):
'THE NAIL HOLES WERE THERE, ALONG WITH THE STRIPS ON HIS BACK'.

When Jesus came down to me, he was smiling at me, he never spoke but his eyes were so deep as if there was a whole world in his eyes.

It was as if his eyes were smiling at me.

In his eyes there was love, understanding, compassion there was also a look and sense that said:

'I know you, you are a true and faithful servant, WELCOME HOME'.

There was a warmth in his eyes that spoke to me and what his eyes also said to me was:

'WELCOME BACK HOME I LOVE YOU AND I HAVE MISSED YOU SO VERY MUCH'.

All this without uttering a word to me.

There was a smile on the face of Jesus, but it was his eyes that spoke to me.

Chapter 5
JESUS WRAPS HIS ARMS AROUND ME

I was pleasantly surprised when Jesus wrapped his arms around me.

Then I was instantly transformed and I felt a love and genuine compassion I had never felt before. It was an instant feeling of indescribable joy, unspeakable joy and love indescribable and unimaginable.

I felt an ocean of love. I felt a peace and joy I have never felt before. I could write a whole library of accolades about this one experience and it would still seem so shallow and small as to my true feelings about what just had happened to me.

It was as if I had spent a lifetime for this one event. A most important event to ever happen to me. (I was going home).

I have heard drug users talk about the perfect high. That was what it was like a perfect high.

The cares and worries of this world simply melted away.
If you were dying of cancer, your house was being foreclosed on and you just lost your job and your wife and kids just left you that all melted away into NOTHING, it didn't matter and you didn't care.

Those things of the world simply melted away from your mind. All you could think about was Jesus and seeing Heaven and how wonderful you felt and how much love you felt and how much you loved also.

This kind of love transcends all boundaries of understanding it's like my tiny 3-pound brain trying to describe God in all his glory, compassion, realm and depth, it just simply cannot be done.

But Lord I am trying.

When Jesus wrapped his arms around me, I felt his arms around me, I felt the weight and the warmth of his arms upon me. I felt Jesus hold me in his arms. Could I describe that to you?   I wish I could, all I can say is that whatever words I could find simply could NOT and would NOT do the experience justice.

When you think you can NOT feel any more love and joy, more is given unto you and then MORE.   It's not the kind of joy that makes you giggle but the kind of joy that strikes you in awe.   And all you want to do is fall down at His feet and worship Him.
It's as if you never realized there was so much love and joy possible.

The things that Satan promises, (but never delivers on), such as life eternal, joy, fulfillment, love, grace, power.

Oh, Satan will give you fame and fortune for a short while here on earth but then it's gone and only after it's too late, ONLY then will you discover it's all a lie. Satan's goal is to deceive, divide, confuse, steal, kill and destroy. (And he's very good at it.)

But God gives you such indescribable joy, peace and unfathomable, limitless, unending love, pure love and Joy Unspeakable.

I could spend a lifetime writing about this one aspect of my Rapture dream it would be about 100 lifetimes too short to even scratch the surface about how Jesus touched me. And yes, He touched me and of that fact you could never convince me otherwise.

When Jesus wrapped his arms around me, I felt everything of this world melt away.

Can anyone honestly and truthful say that:

THEY KNOW WHAT IT FEELS LIKE TO BE IN THE ARMS OF JESUS? TO BE HELD IN THE ARMS OF THE CREATOR, THE ONE WHO MADE THE WHOLE UNIVERSE AND EVERYTHING IN IT?

I THINK I KNOW.   BUT WORDS FALL FAR SHORT OF BEING ABLE TO DESCRIBE THIS TO YOU.

I THINK THIS YOU WILL HAVE TO TAKE ON FAITH.   THAT ALL YOUR TRIALS AND TRIBULATIONS HERE ON THIS EARTH WILL BE REWARDED AND THE REWARD WILL FAR SURPASS YOUR EARTHLY TRIALS.

TRUST IN GOD FOR HE IS FAITHFUL AND TRUE AND HIS WORDS WILL LAST FOREVER.

Chapter 6
MY GLORIFIED NEW BODY

One thing that happened the instant that Jesus put his arms around me I felt a change in my body. I noticed how my eyesight was now sharp again, my old rickety body was transformed and new, with no more pain, no more suffering. No more tears, no more heartache, no more strife.

The things of this world simply melted away. I felt a joy, peace and a love like I had never felt before.   In the twinkling of an eye I was transformed, I was changed into a glorified beautiful new body.

And if you are like me and a little overweight, you will be trim and fit in your new body.   In your new glorified body, everything will be perfect.   I felt like I was back in my 20's again.

NO MATTER WHAT your problems on this earth were, or are they simply melted away and not just from your worry but from your memory as well. You found that you couldn't remember anything that worried, confounded or confused you.

You had an instant understanding how and why things were the way they were. You had an instant knowledge and understanding and an instant renewal of not only your body but your mind and your soul is now finally set FREE within your new glorified body.

I had the feeling that I could do almost anything, go anywhere, if I wanted to zip off to Alpha Centaur to see the Nubile or to see a massive star go super nova it was only about a second in flight time.   And NO, I did not try this out, it was just how I felt.

Remember the Bible says a thousand years with the Lord in Heaven is as a day and a day is as a thousand years.

We here on this earth have time and clocks, but time in Heaven doesn't mean anything, there are no clocks in Heaven.   Time has no meaning in Heaven. In Heaven you live outside of time and space.

I have heard people talk about being or feeling like Super Man, that was how I felt. But I didn't need to flaunt it, I just knew it. Besides everyone else felt just like me, it all felt so natural.

It felt like I remember this, it felt like this is the way things are supposed to be. I felt like I was a stranger in a strange land who finally came home.

And home is where you are at in that place.

Things were revealed to me, they were just made known to me. And if I had a question it was answered or made known to me immediately. I had a lot of questions but I had more pressing things to experience before I got to my questions.

The closest I can describe it in simple terms in which I think most can or will understand it is:

'Being a 'two-year-old' and safe and warm nestled in your loving and protective Mother's arms. Where you know you are safe, warm, where nothing in the world could ever harm you, safe, secure and loved beyond measure.'

To be honest this is one dream I wish I had kept on having.   Honestly what I felt was indescribable.

It would be like ancient man describing to his friend a 747 flying low overhead.

There are no words, there is no means of properly conveying exactly what I saw and what I felt.

And my feeble words could NEVER do the experience justice.

But what I DID experience was life changing, life altering.   When I woke up I knew I had heard from God and God gave me something VERY special.

Before my Rapture dream, I rarely watched Rapture dream videos on youtube.   It was not because I didn't believe them, but that most of these people having Rapture dreams were having highly subjective dreams that were more in the interpretation than in actual substance.

For example, and I am NOT quoting any ones dream and I am NOT making fun of any one's dream, but I am simply making an observation here.

Say someone has a dream where a squirrel runs across the street followed by 4 other squirrels and they all run up a tree to safety. A dream like that doesn't really tell me anything it's all left up to the dreamer as to how to interpret the dream.

NOW that said if that dream was followed with scripture or a message from the Holy Spirit that would give strong evidence that it was a Holy Spirit inspired dream.   But now the question begs was it meant just for you or were you meant to share the dream with others.   For those questions I would only say to be led by the Holy Spirit and be faithful.

BUT my Rapture dream was not subjective or left to interpretation it was an IN YOUR FACE dream that needed no explanation or interpretation and it needed no confirmation the dream itself WAS the confirmation.

I have had many powerful and emotional dreams about the Tribulation. BUT this Rapture dream was the most perfect, the most emotional, the most direct in your face dream that was full of not only emotion.

It was full of color and feelings, you felt things from your senses such as sight, touch, feel, smell and hear and it was ALL there.

Another aspect that was very unusual about my dream is that I had never had a dream where I felt so much love and pure joy, in my dream.

And then you had other things that were NOT from your senses: emotion, love, joy, contentment, being truly happy but now these emotions were amplified by a million times.

Chapter 7
NOW I KNOW WHAT IT WILL FEEL LIKE TO BE IN HEAVEN

I think I truly know what it will feel like in Heaven.   With all I have described about how I felt when Jesus wrapped his loving arms around me. Now I think I truly know.

A lot of people think Heaven is where you sit on a cloud for eternity playing a harp.

No wonder why so many people are not interested in going to Heaven.

God took 6 days to make the earth, sun, moon, the universe and everything in it.   Have you ever seen photos of Galaxies off in distant space and seen how breathtaking and beautiful they are?

Well God did all that in 6 days just think how much more beautiful Heaven will be because God had over 2000 years to make Heaven PERFECT for the Saints.

And NO, you will not be sitting on a cloud playing a harp, (unless you really want to).   Everyone will have a job in Heaven but it's not like a job of sweat and toil, but more a labor of love, something satisfying and fulfilling.

It will be something you will love to do and you will not have a boss, you will not have a time clock, again your job will be a labor of love and you will be loved for doing it too.

There will be indescribable beauty, flowers, trees, a lake, a stream and many mansions prepared for us. The colors will be indescribable as well as the intensity of the colors. The lake and the flowing stream will be like looking at flowing crystal glass.   There will be feasts and indescribable foods.

There will be no sun there, we will receive our light and warmth radiating from God the Father.   His light will light our world and there shall be no more darkness, no more clouds, no more dreary days for every day will be perfect as God is Perfect, Holy and True.

(NOW this part I did not dream but it's from the Bible and from trusted sources that have said this and I believe it to be so.)

Some people will ask; 'Do our pets go to Heaven'? That I cannot say definitively, remember I was only Raptured and Transformed and I never saw Heaven.   But based on others who I trust who have had dreams and Near-Death Experiences they saw animals in Heaven and the Bible says the Lion will lie down with the lamb. So, I believe our pets go to Heaven and like us they also will be in glorified bodies.

The closest thing I can use to describe how I felt was I felt a little like Super Man but in a righteous and glorious way. I felt like I was finally going home. Not to some place foreign and strange but home.

Like I belonged there, it was like I came from there, I was lost and now I am found.   And all I could think about was the love and the thought of going home.   Home is a wonderful place, a place you belong, a place of rest a place where everyone loves you.

A place of peace and contentment, a place of pure love and indescribable joy.

Oh, how I long to go home!

Remember this: That with the shed blood of Jesus Christ we are no longer servants.   But we now are Sons and Daughters (heirs and joint heirs) of the most high God.

There is one item I left out of this until now and that is:
When you receive your Glorified body, you will discover that there is NO MORE SIN, there is Not even a word for sin. It's all washed away.

The very idea, thought and meaning of sin will escape from you and there will be no more sin. Joy unspeakable and full of glory.
Now that is the power of God at work.

In this world we are continually bombarded with sin from every angle and every means.   Most people recognize sin in movies, television, books etc. But now we are bombarded daily and ceaselessly with sin from unrecognized sources.

Did you know the very air you breath, the food you eat and the water you drink is now full of abominations to God. They are doing high altitude spraying of metals and chemicals for whatever reason. There are those who say that they are even high altitude spraying of DNA.

In the last days Satan will run to and FRO creating as much havoc as he can because he knows his time grows short. So, putting DNA even Nephilim DNA in our food and water is something Satan and his henchmen would do in a heartbeat. So, do I believe it, sadly yes, I do.

I also received a warning that not all food was safe to eat. And I was reminded to say the Blessing over every meal.   Satan cannot stay in anything blessed in Jesus name.

Remember God Is In Control.

I don't like talking doom and gloom, but it seems that most churches are afraid to talk about what is coming. They don't want to offend young people who are planning on going to college and raise a family, buy a house and a car, get married, have children and have so much of life to look forward to.

I sometimes think people look at me and think that I want to take all that away from them.

The truth is I do not want to take anything away from anyone.

But I am here to tell you that if you are Raptured your life is 'THEN' just beginning.

You then have an eternity to look forward too without any of the problems of this world like finding a job, marriage, divorce, sickness, death, operations, doctors, growing old, old age pains, having to work to provide for a family, not a tear, not a memory of pain or suffering.   God will wipe away every tear and every strife from each and every heart.

As we will be going home. Home a place you belong, a place you came from but forgot.   A place of peace, security, tranquility and much love. A place of indescribable beauty. A place where the streets are paved with gold.   And there is so much love and compassion there that it is indescribable love, beauty and joy. As you are completely wrapped up in Jesus arms, safe and loved forever.

In my Rapture dream Jesus came down to me and he put his arms around me. I wish there were words to describe how I felt being in the arms of Jesus.   All I can say about that is that I was in the arms of God and I felt boundless, endless love and compassion.

Also, what I remember was that he never spoke a word to me but his eyes spoke volumes to me. What I saw in his eyes was pure love, a love that transcends everything known about love, a love without bounds or depths.

God will wipe away every tear and every strife from each and every heart. All you will feel is love and joy unspeakable.

A place where the streets are paved with gold.   And there is so much love and compassion there that it is indescribable love and joy.

The eyes of Jesus not only showed the love he had for me, they said something else to me; And what his eye said was:

'I HAVE MISSED YOU SO VERY MUCH, WELCOME HOME'.

I wish I had never woken up from that dream and now I will spend the rest of my time (on this earth) trying to get back to the place where I was before HOME!

Remember when you were a kid and a jet flew high overhead? Remember the vapor trail it followed the jet but quickly dissipated, it followed the jet up to a mile or a little less.

But today you see those normal vapor trails but you also see vapor trails where they go from horizon to horizon and spread out like a cloud. And now you see multiple vapor trails crisscross the sky as if they are saturating an area. Do you ever wonder what are they doing and what are they spraying on the population below?

The water you drink even if it's bottled water, it's the chemicals in the packaging that leaches into the water or the chemicals they put in the water.

And if it's not that then it's the fact that water treatment plants put chemicals IN your drinking water and some of these chemicals are NON- APPROVED drugs. This makes your local water company responsible for dosing everyone with non-approved drugs.

They arrest your neighbor for selling (non-approved) drugs but your water company is exempt from these laws.

And can anyone tell me the recommended dose of fluoride for children, infants, toddlers and the elderly?   No, you cannot and neither can your water company.

And if that were not enough water treatment plants do not have the means or facilities to filter out antidepressants, stimulants, hormones, herbicides, pesticides, insecticides, DNA and a whole host of other drugs and chemicals.

DO YOU KNOW what is in your air, food, water and drinks?   Today with GMO's, animal and human DNA, HEK293 exotic chemicals you don't know what you are eating and drinking and if you knew 'you would be shocked'.   This is all part of Satan's end of days plan, his strategy.

[]   []
Matthew 24: 22
And except those days should be shortened, there should be no flesh be saved: but for the elect's sake those days shall be shortened.

The scriptures before this verse are pre-rapture verses, so this must be a pre-rapture verse.

Do you understand what God is saying here?   With all the abominations (sin) in our food, water and our air God is going to have to shorten his coming or there will be NO FLESH LEFT TO SAVE!

What the Glorified Body is, it is a gift from God more precious than all the gold, all the silver and all the precious stones of the earth.

Along with all the end of days signs if you read Matthew 24 it's a shopping list of end of days signs and we are now seeing every single one of these signs being fulfilled today. Yes, Time Is Short.

One of the latest signs to be fulfilled is that for the first time in over 2000 years a perfect red Heifer has been born in Israel. You say: 'so what, what kind of sign is this'?

The perfect red Heifer calf 3 years old is what is sacrificed 'IN THE TEMPLE' in Jerusalem for sin.

As in the third Temple that has been prophesied but not yet built. But it will be soon and now they have the perfect sacrifice for their new temple.

The red Heifer must be sacrificed before the calf turns 3 years old. This age limit starts from inception NOT from birth, so that only gives us about 2 years. Contractors say the temple can be built in as little as 12 to 18 months.

The Jews have been busy building the altar and everything else that goes into the temple, all they need is the physical structure.

YOUR TIME HERE
DRAWETH NEIGH

Recently a new end times sign has just appeared as prophesied in Ezekiel 47:10 fish have returned to the Dead Sea. This is recognized as an end of days prophesy coming true right now.

Even the vague prophecy of Lamentations 5: 18
Now foxes have been photographed walking on the Western Wall in Jerusalem. This prophecy speaks of the return of the Messiah very soon after foxes are seen running and playing on the Western Wall.

So now even the vague and seemingly inconsequential prophecies are coming true. How much longer oh Lord, how much longer?

But until that blessed day and that blessed hour, I will be watching for his coming to Rapture his faithful from this wicked and vile place.

The Dead Sea is the lowest point on earth and it is the saltiest body of water on the earth, so how is it there are fish in the Dead Sea? I don't know but the Bible says it, so I believe it, and now it is so.

Just one more sign that we are living in the last days, the last hours, the last minutes before we who are faithful and true are Raptured out of here. And then the real pain and suffering will begin for those left behind in the Tribulation.

We are going home soon, VERY SOON.

Our work and toil here will end one day soon.

Our well-deserved rest and reward will come at last.

Our fight and our struggle will be over

We who are faithful will receive our reward.

We will go home soon.

Home that word means a place familiar, a place you know. Not a foreign or unfamiliar or strange place, but a place you know, a place you call HOME.

Home a place where you finally can rest, a place of peace and security.

A place you feel like you know, a place where you came FROM a place you are returning to,

a place you call HOME.

What sticks out in my mind was the feeling of pure love, undiluted love, love beyond comprehension or belief it was joy unspeakable and I was most excited to be going HOME at last.

Another thing I felt, knew or sensed was the fact there was no more sin and not just (NO SIN), there was not even a word for sin. Sin was gone, even the knowledge of sin was removed from me. I felt pure love and grace from Jesus who put his arms around me.   I felt pure love from Jesus.

Another thing I realized was I had no more pain. I live in and with constant pain with my left knee. I went on a trip with a group of senior citizens one day to Paris Arkansas to the Coal Miners Museum. It was very interesting and if you ever get the chance you should take the tour as it was great and exciting.

I noticed out of our group of about 15 I had the most difficulty walking and I had to sit down about every 5 or 10 minutes. Luckily, they had lots of benches there. But I was the one who had the most difficult time walking and standing with my knee pain.

If anyone had an excuse to not get on his or her knees to pray it would be me. But as hard and as difficult as it is for me, I get on my knees to pray, I will get on my knees. My wife tells me that God knows how difficult it is for me to get on my knees and God does not require me to get on my knees.

I know, God does not ask or require me to get on my knees before him. As long as I have one good knee, I will get on my knees before almighty God. When God no longer wants me to get on my knees God will tell me.

For me as long as I can get on my knees, I will.
I will humble myself before almighty God the Alpha and the Omega, from everlasting to everlasting, without beginning and without end.

Because my God is the One and Only true living God.
The God of Abraham, the God of Isaac, the God of Jacob and the God of Moses.

I do not tell you this to brag, I think we all need to humble ourselves before God in whatever way we can.

Because when you lower yourself, you uplift God.

What a mighty God we serve.

Chapter 8
IDEAS TO PROMOTE YOUR CHURCH

This was so much more than a dream. It was a message from God reminding me (us) just a glimpse of what we gain by following Jesus Christ.

I had a dream also where I was commanded to: 'WAKE UP AND TELL THE PEOPLE'.

And since then I have been working diligently in the Lord, speaking at my church, speaking on the radio, talking to people, writing books, articles, building and updating my website, making youtube videos, mailing letters to churches and so much more.

But I DO NOT do this for my glory but to glorify the one who sent me (Jesus Christ). As there is no other name in heaven or on earth that can save you, me or anyone from what is shortly to come upon this vile and wicked earth.

I DO NOT tell you this to brag but to only give you ideas that you can possibly do for your church. I print up church business cards for our church with the church logo and name and address on it. I also have the times of the various services our church has also listed on the card.

Along with that I have our pastors name and I welcome everyone to 'Worship God With Us'. PLEASE DO NOT include your pastors phone number (without permission). If your church has a dedicated phone line (that a live person answers the phone) you may want to include that phone number. But you need to ask first before printing any cards.

I inform the congregation at my church that they all need to carry 10 or 12 cards with them at all times. This way if the Holy Spirit moves upon you to talk to someone about the saving grace of Jesus Christ you will have a church business card to hand them.

When you are in any business that has a public poster board you can post a church business card. If you are eating out you will notice a lot of businesses will drop off 6 or 7 cards near the cash register. This will be a great place to drop off several cards. You always ask first and then you will only drop off 6 or 7 cards.

The reason being, some people (for whatever reason) when they see a stack of church cards will pick them ALL up. And you may speak to one lady behind the cash register and she says YES but then you have a shift change or the restaurant closes for the night and your cards (can) disappear.

You will find a lot of businesses will have a public post board for everyone to post business cards to lost pet notices to local small business. I guess the business sees this as a way of promoting local businesses and churches.

A good cheap place to order church business cards is a company called Vista Print. You can find them on line at: www.vistaprint.com
They have an online program where you can pick out a logo and build your business card right on line. I have used them several times and I find them highly reputable.

The local post office has a local mailing option where you can mail a printed piece of literature to every address in your area it's called 'Every Door Direct Mail'.

If you are interested in doing a local mailing this a great way to do it without having to do a 'bulk' mailing and having to have a permit and all of that. And weather it's a post card type of mailing or a full page 8 ½ by 11.

A very ingenious way you can get your mailing for free is to run your ad on one side and charge other local small business owners a small fee for advertising on the reverse of your mailing.

If you are doing a piece that is 8 ½ by 11 then you can run 4 to 6 ads on the reverse side of your mailing and just charge enough to cover your expenses for your side of the mailing including postage & printing. That is how you can get your mailing for FREE.

I am not talking about a way to 'make money' but only enough to cover your printing and postage expenses. That way their price for advertising on your flier will be cheap and they will not have a good excuse not to advertise on your flier.

A word of caution, being you are doing a church mailing you do NOT want advertisers on your mailing who are promoting liquor, beer and wine stores. Or tobacco shops and the like.

To promote a local small market will be OK as long as the AD they are promoting does not mention tobacco products or beer, wine or any liquor products. PLEASE keep in mind you DO NOT want to promote Jesus on one side of your flier and Satan on the other.

Another thing I have done for my church is I had made up yard signs (like the small yard signs politicians have made up when they are running to get elected) You can find these companies on the internet. I think the company I used was called www.signsonthecheap.com

They have a program where you can build your yard sign right on the internet including any artwork you want to include. As for my sign I had a cross for the art work.

You can get yard signs printed up advertising your church and then pass them out at your church. And you can end up with 10, 20 even 50 yard signs promoting your church all over town.

These are just a couple ideas that you can use to promote your church locally. I am sure that you can think of others

After all WE are Promoting something, we have something to offer the public. Our product is desperately needed by everyone.

I once prayed and I asked God how I could promote the church and just what I could say and what I could NOT say.

The Holy Spirit told me that I could do anything and say anything that was truthful, honest, with love, scriptural and pleasing to God. If you think about it that opens lots of doors to us and it closes very few doors to us. Let the Holy Spirit be your guide.

If you say something in an ad that you are not 100% positive that the Holy Spirit approves, then sleep and pray hard on it first before you commit to it and it cost you money.

Remember Satan will try to trick you, to get you to say something that is not quite right or to promote a beer and wine ad on the back of your mailing or some such action.   Do Not Do It – and if you are not sure about something then pray on it for guidance from the Holy Spirit.

Chapter 9
MY CONCLUSION WITH ALL THIS

I have been blessed beyond measure and my blessings number as the stars and I think God for each and every blessing he has bestowed upon me.

My Conclusion in this is that there is NO conclusion in Jesus Christ.
Our time upon this earth is but a mist and a vapor. If you don't think so, let me ask you, when did you graduate from high school, get married? When did you have your first child? How old are they now? How old are you now?

The point is our time here is quickly gone and our allotted time here is supposed to be for God's glory (not ours). And since our time here is so short that makes us all missionaries in the work of Jesus Christ.

And one day we will be going home, to our permanent home in Paradise.

We are to be a peculiar people unto Jesus Christ apart from the world. WE live in this world but we are to be apart FROM this world.

Our purpose and reason here on this earth is this:

WE ARE TO GLORIFY AND WORSHIP GOD

WITH EVERY STEP WE TAKE

WITH EVERY BREATH WE TAKE

WITH EVERY WORD WE UTTER

We are here for God's purpose

For God's Pleasure – AND NOT OURS.

For God will do all his pleasure.

I have been shown powerful and disturbing dreams and with these dreams I have wept bitterly.   I have cried and sobbed so hard like when you lose a child or your Mother passes away. I have wept that hard over some of these dreams and visions that I have been shown.

My wife would walk in on me crying and concerned she would ask 'Why are you crying'   and all I could say was: 'I know what is coming' and on another occasion I told her that: 'A lot of people are going to get hurt'.

But then the Holy Spirit showed me this verse:

Matthew 24: 6
And ye shall hear of wars and rumors of wars: see that ye be not troubled: for all these things must come to pass, but the end is not yet.

Your Mother who carried you in her womb and protected you and who bore you through labor pains.   Who nursed you, who cared for, changed your diapers, who kept you warm and comfortable who held you in her arms protecting you and kissing your hurts.   Who was always there for you.

God is so much closer than that to you. After all who placed you IN your Mother's womb? Who gave you THAT Mother?

(If you had a mother who was not all those things or if you had no mother than I am truly sorry, BUT that does not negate the fact that God still loves you)

Yes, my Rapture dream was the most powerful and emotional dream I have ever had.   And after that dream I will spend the rest of my time here on this earth to do the will of Jesus Christ.

I will do anything and everything to guarantee that I get BACK to that place that I was once in.

To get back to that feeling of pure joy, grace and boundless love.

You may ask would I lay down my life?   YES, if it be God's will because I know, I have seen only a glimpse of what lies on the other side.   Remember this life or time on this earth is but a mist and a vapor and then it's gone.

But our time in heaven will be boundless, endless, limitless with so much peace, joy and love you will find it hard to comprehend just how FULL it is and it will be without end, forever and forever.

So that means after a few hundred trillion years it will be as if we have just begun. I figure it will take that long to discover all there is to see and experience in heaven and if that were not enough some things will change and seem to become brand new again over and over. Nothing is ever the same it seems. Everything will be brand new.

If you were blind, your eyes will be restored in heaven.

If you had missing arms or legs you will get them back in heaven.

No one wears glasses in heaven.

No one wears hearing aids in heaven.

Everyone looks to be in their 20's or maybe late 20's.

Yes, babies are Raptured, even babies from their Mother's womb will be Raptured. But in heaven these babies will be as 7, 8 or 9 years old. They will be wise beyond their years and they will be filled with the Spirit of God.

There will be no pain, no suffering and never ever a tear in heaven.

Old things have passed away and everything will be brand new.

And no matter how much you deny, disbelieve or disprove God and his word the KJV Bible that will never (NOT make it right). And what the Bible says is coming upon this earth, you can bet IT IS COMING. And no amount of rejection or disbelief will ever UN-do what is coming.

There are a lot of religions that have their own version of their own bible. But here is the thing, a truth that is undeniable. These other bibles (religious books) DO NOT prophesy, they do not tell you what is coming, THE BIBLE DOES. That is your proof right there that the KJV Bible is the inspired true word of God.

There are over 1500 prophesy's in the KJV Bible. Many of these prophecies are 2,600 years old and older. These prophecies were written and many years later they were fulfilled just as the Bible said they would.

Every single prophesy has been fulfilled exactly as the Bible said it would. The prophecies of Jesus' birth, life, crucifixion, death. Burial and resurrection have ALL been fulfilled by Jesus. SO, what are the odds that the remaining few prophecies of the end of days will not be fulfilled literally and exactly as written in the Bible?

Chapter 10
THE MILLENNIAL REIGN

People seem to forget the Millennial Reign of Jesus Christ on the earth that will last for 1000 years upon this earth.

The book of Revelation tells about all kinds of terrible plagues and suffering that will come over the earth in the end of days. God's wrath will be poured out and Satan's wrath will also be poured out upon the earth. This time in history will be called the Great Tribulation.

The Rapture will come first and then the Tribulation will begin. As long as sin is in the world the earth will become steadily more corrupt and more vile.

But at Jesus Second Coming (after the Rapture) and at the end of the Tribulation Jesus will return with the armies of heaven and after the battle of Armageddon there will begin a glorious time of healing upon the earth.

This will be the beginning of the Millennial Reign upon the earth. And they shall beat their swords into pruning hooks and plows.

The Millennial Reign is a time of peace upon the earth when Jesus will reign on the throne in Jerusalem and the Saints will rule in righteousness. In this time all wrongs will be corrected. And evil will be abolished from the earth.

Isaiah 65: 20 – 25 Describes this period. What these verses say is that the Millennial Reign we will all be farmers tending our small part of the Garden of Eden (if you will) and that we will only grow what we need and no more.

No one will steal or murder and no one will exploit another. The earth will be ruled by Jesus Christ, his bride and the martyrs. Revelation 20: 4 And their governing will be fair, honest and true according to God's laws.

It will be how God always intended the earth to be in the first place. Creation in complete harmony with its creator the way the Garden of Eden was intended to be.

People will live longer Isaiah 65: 20 Even the animals will stop killing and eating each other. As then all animals will eat grass and plants. As the lion shall lie down with the lamb. Isaiah 65: 25.

Chapter 11
MY EYES WERE OPENED

I must be honest with you; I have never been to heaven. But when I was Raptured, I gained a keen sense of just what it will feel like IN Heaven in my dream.

When Jesus placed his arms around me and held me in his arms I was instantly transformed. I became a new person. My body was changed in the twinkling of an eye. I was no longer in a physical body but I had obtained a spiritual body.

It is hard to describe just how this felt. On one hand I felt I still had physical characteristics, I was still me but changed and I knew it. I was not like a wisp of smoke or like you could see through me. I had solid physical body but that body had changed somehow. As if I was both physical and spiritual at the same time.

I still felt with my senses. I still saw things. But I was changed I had no more pain, no more painful memories. All the old life just melted away. The old earthly life and the old earthly body just melted away into nothing, not even a memory.

The funny thing is, say you had cancer and was lying on your death bed and you got Raptured from your death bed. That would all just melt away into nothing as nothing of this earth has any meaning there.

I saw with new eyes as if the scales had been removed. I felt young again, I felt strong, I felt invigorated, I was a new creature in Jesus Christ all over again.

I felt an overpowering love, a love without bounds and without reason. A love that could never be measured. If you ever felt a little over weight, a little homely or maybe even a little ugly.

That had no meaning in this place as Jesus loves us all the same as we are all beautiful to him.   And Jesus loved us so much that he died for us.   God loved us that much.

When I saw Jesus face to face in my Rapture dream, he never spoke a word. But what his eyes said spoke volumes.   What I saw in his eyes was the pure love he had for me.   But what I saw more than this was: 'I HAVE MISSED YOU SO VERY MUCH, WELCOME BACK HOME'.

Home a place you know, a place you came from, a place you are returning to, a place where you feel love, peace, joy and security.   A place where the joy and love are without bounds, un-measurable, unfathomable, without end and beyond reason or understanding.

Home a place where you are loved beyond measure. Where joy unspeakable is every day and every second. Where you will experience a peace and love you have never known before. And you will feel secure as there are no locks in heaven. No one ever locks a door in heaven.

Another thing that is missing is sin, as there in heaven there is no sin and not even a word for sin. On earth I know you are tempted and tested all the time and sin and temptation is everywhere. But in heaven there is no more sin.

Yes, I did receive a new glorified body when I was Raptured but only for a moment. But in that moment, I truly think I felt what it will feel like in heaven. Everyone there will have a new glorified spiritual body. Everyone there will feel like you. In heaven there will not be any old people, no gray hair and no one wears glasses in heaven.

Now I may be off a few years on this but not by much. No one in heaven is (or appears to be) any older than about 25 to 28 years old. So, if you had a grandmother who passed on to be with the Lord at 95 years old, in heaven she would look only to be around 25 years old.

You would think with all the abortions all over the world and all the children that have died very young that heaven would be one giant nursery.

But you would be wrong, even aborted babies will appear to be about 7 or 8 years old. They will be childlike in looks only as they also will have great wisdom and reasoning just as the adults and all with a glorified body.

Yes, I was given a glorified spiritual body but there was so much more. I felt I knew things, that all things were or would be revealed to me. But when I came back into this earthly body, when the dream ended, all that was taken from me.

I felt like IF I had a question it would be instantly revealed to me. I felt like I would instantly just know the answer. In heaven all things that are secret will be reveled. That also was taken from me when I came back.

Yes my eyes were opened and the scales were removed and I saw things, wondrous marvelous things and that was only being Raptured. How much more marvelous could heaven be?

Chapter 12
WHAT WILL WE FEEL LIKE IN HEAVEN

Again, I tell you I have not been to Heaven. But the Holy Spirit has revealed things about heaven and so I am telling you.

When I received my glorified body, I did not sense this, but the Holy Spirit

revealed it to me. That when everyone gets their glorified body they become as Supermen, with super human strength, wisdom and other power.

But if you remember the Superman movies, what made Superman special was the fact he was the only one who had super powers. But in heaven we all will have super powers and since we all will have these super powers we all will have the same abilities so we all will be the same and no one will be different or special.

I do not know what all these powers will be, I just know we will have powers. I know say for instance we want to fly off to the Crab Nebula and witness a quasar go Super Nova (explode). The distance may be 20 Billion light years. But for us it may only be a 5 second flight.

And we will need no propulsion system, no life support, we will simply fly away and be there. Then when we get their we may get say a million miles away from the Quasar and when it explodes it will be brighter than the entire Universe for only a few seconds and spew trillions upon trillions of cubic miles of matter, radiation and harmful emissions of all kind in all directions. But nothing will harm us or even bother us, as we are spiritual beings.

You will not require rest or sleep. I know the Bible says 'In my Father's house are many mansions (or rooms) but believe me you will not need a room to sleep in. It is there only because God said he was going away to prepare you a place and that where He was you would be also.

You will not require food, but we will all set at the Banquet table and partake.   But you will not need sustenance as your sustenance comes from God himself.

You will not require sunlight for light and warmth.   As our light and warmth shall come from the glory of the Father.   As His glory is our light and our warmth forevermore.

We are not married in heaven as we are all the bride of Jesus Christ in Heaven.   As for male and female that question is without meaning in a glorified spiritual body.   So, when a woman gets Raptured do, they keep their hair, fair complexion and other feminine traits?

I have not received any clarification on this.   But I personally believe a female will keep feminine traits and a man will keep masculine traits, but keep in mind that whatever age you are if you are older you will be in your mid to later 20's in heaven.

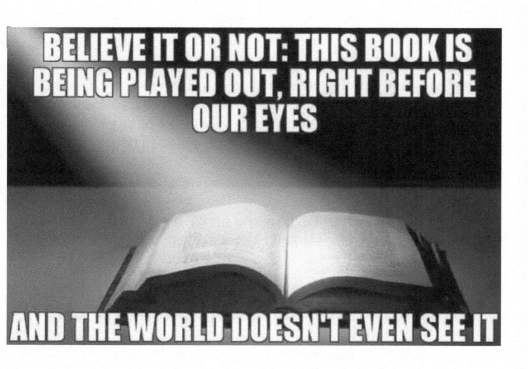

You cannot procreate in heaven, you will not need to use the bathroom in heaven, so no reproductive organs are in heaven or maybe they just do not work in heaven, (I am not clear on this).

If that is a concern for you than maybe you should search out your motives for going to heaven and pray on it real hard.   Besides what are the alternatives, there are none except to enter the Tribulation.

It is not that God is against sex after all he made us, like we are here on earth to procreate.   But in a glorified body you will be like the angels in heaven. You will be a spiritual being and as such you will not have sex or even the ability to have sex or procreate.

When you get Raptured out of here, if you have any implants, body jewelry or a total knee implant you will leave all that behind.   Any part of your body that is altered, fake, implants, tattoos, everything of the like you will leave behind.

When you receive your glorified spiritual body, you will leave everything earthly behind you. Any implants will be left behind you will have new knees, new hips even new teeth nothing of this earth will follow you.

If you have a prosthetic limb you will leave that behind as well, as your spiritual body will be complete with no missing parts. So, if you have missing or damaged eyes, limbs, fingers they will all be replaced with new body parts.   Remember no one in heaven wears glasses, so no one in heaven has any missing body parts.   We will all be complete in heaven in spiritual bodies.

You will have eternal life without sin and since Satan is removed the tempter, liar and great deceiver will be gone.   There will be no more sin, more than that there will not even be a word for sin.

In your new glorified body, you will be like Jesus in spirit form and with all manner of power.   But you will have limits to your power.   For instance there is one place you cannot go to visit and that place is hell.

You will not be allowed to visit or view hell.   There are other powers you will not have; you will not have the power to create life, planets, suns, or worlds, or heaven, hell or earth or procreate.

You will not have the ability to create living things.   That power is reserved for God and God alone.

As for the power to create music, songs, poetry anything that glorifies Jesus you will enjoy all those kinds of things.

As to exactly what power I cannot say.

When we receive our new glorified spiritual body our relationship with Jesus changes.   In our old flesh body, we were humble servants.

But after we receive our spiritual body we are accepted more like a brother and a sister as we will be in a spirit body just like Jesus and we will be more like Him than ever before.   We will be removed from sin and sin will be removed from us so then we can be accepted closer to the throne. At that point our status will be above the angels of heaven.

There are no back pews in heaven, not like church.   If you expect to get to heaven and get lost in the crowd, you are mistaken.   There are no back pews in heaven, in fact there are no pews at all.

Everyone is up front; everyone has an up close and personal relationship with Jesus Christ.   So, if you have been the kind of person who sits on the back pew and tosses in some change in the offering plate, never went to the altar, never sang, never testified and sneaks out when the service is over you may need to re-think that.

In heaven everyone joins in worshiping God, everyone sings, everyone shouts Holy, Holy, Holy art thou oh Lord.   No one sits that out.   So, if you are a bench warmer in church you need to get off the fence (bench) and join in and glorify God now just to get in practice.   Because in heaven everyone joins in and no one sits on a back pew in heaven.

When I was transformed into a spiritual being it was wondrous joyful process and it took only the twinkling of an eye.   But in my case it happened when Jesus came down to me and placed his arms around me.

The transformation was instantaneous and without any fanfare (except for being in the arms of Jesus) as for what I felt of that process, at first I was not even aware that I had changed but I then noticed I felt different, I thought different, I loved more, I saw through new eyes, I felt with a new heart.   I knew that I had been changed into a glorified spiritual body.

Chapter 13
WHAT WILL IT LOOK LIKE IN HEAVEN

If God made such astounding beauty on this earth and in this Universe in just 6 days, just imagine how much more beautiful heaven will be since God had thousands of years to make heaven perfect for us.

There is mention in Revelation 4: 6 of a Crystal Sea like glass.   I would suppose that no matter how deep you looked into the Crystal Sea you could still see the bottom as it would be that clear.   If there is a sea there must be a beach, a shore line and most likely palm trees.

Though I have never seen heaven there are a few people who I trust who have seen heaven and what they say is that nothing can compare with heaven.   The majesty, the colors, everything stays in bloom and the colors are so vibrant and vivid they almost hurt your eyes to look upon them.

There are fruit trees of all varieties everywhere that are always bearing beautiful and delicious fruit.   All plants keep their leaves all the time. And plant leaves are normally green but in heaven there are every color of leaves you can imagine.

Nothing ever looks soiled, dirty or used, everything always looks brand new. There is no wear and tear on anything ever.   Everything stays like it was never used. So, everything always looks brand new.

There are never any weeds or pests like ants or flies to bother us.   As we are in spirit form, we cannot be bothered any way.   Everyone is in spirit form in heaven.

If your idea of heaven is palm trees and a beach that is what you will see and where you will be. But if your idea of heaven is a log cabin n the woods on a stream then that is what you will see. So, heaven is something different for everyone. You say how can this be?

The truth is I do not know all things. I only know what I was shown and what I was told. I was not given any reasons or explanations for how things work. I guess heaven has to be taken on faith. On this I have one more thing to say and that is God is God and God can do anything, everything except lie or fail.

You may ask:
'Is there fishing in heaven'? That is a good question and I wish I knew the answer. But something tells me that 'IF' there is fishing in heaven it's strictly 'catch and release'.

Chapter 14
PETS IN HEAVEN

I know a lot of people have the same question: 'Will my pets go to heaven also?'

To be very frank and honest, I cannot definitively say. BUT I can say this, there are animals in heaven. These animals are in spiritual bodies also, so you do not have to worry about flea collars, and the mess pets leave behind. There will be no unpleasant odors, no shedding. All animals will be very well behaved in heaven.

I wish I could give you a definitive answer. But not all things are revealed to me.

I have pets also and for my wife and I it is hard to imagine them being left behind. All I can tell you to do is pray on it. But here is the dilemma in that, if you find yourself praying for your pets more than praying for your loved ones, family, friends, neighbors.

DO YOU SEE A PROBLEM HERE? I think it's fine to pray for your pets, I know that I have. But when you pray more for your pets then you do for your family, neighbors, friends and so on then you have a very serious problem.

If you pray more for your pets than you do for others, do you think that will please God? God expects you to love your pets but God expects you to love your neighbor more, much more. You really need to be praying for your family, friends and neighbors first, then include your pets.

I will go one step further, you need to put your prayers into action and actually talk to your family, neighbors and friends about the love of Jesus and how he died for their sins. Are you working in Jesus Christ? Do you pick up your cross and follow Jesus? It's easy to SAY a thing but much more difficult to do it.

Colton Burpo had a near death experience of going to heaven at 3 years old. He and his Father wrote a book called 'Heaven Is Real' .
In this book Colton saw his sister who had died in her mother's womb and she was about 6, 7 or 8 years old.   She introduced herself to Colton.

Colton also saw his Grandfather who was older when he passed away and wore glasses, but in heaven his Grandfather did not wear glasses and was in his 20's or at least in his early 30's.

Also, Colton saw animals in heaven.

I know I seem to draw a lot from a 3-year old's dream, vision, NDE (whatever you want to call it.)   But keep this in mind a 3-year-old is innocent and has no ulterior motives in what he says and tells people.

Besides there were many others who have had similar experiences.

Chapter 15
WE ALL HAVE A JOB IN HEAVEN

Some people wonder and ask: 'Will we have a job in Heaven?'

The short answer is YES!
We will all have a job in heaven, but it will not be like any job you could imagine and it's not like digging ditches or cleaning toilets. It will be something fulfilling, uplifting, inspiring and something you love to do.

Something we will have a passion to do. Something we will love to do. For example, my wife has stated over and over that in heaven she wanted to work with children. I am sure in heaven she will get her wish.

But it will not be like a normal job where you punch a time clock and work until it's break time or lunch. And finding yourself watching the clock until it's time to punch out. Even if you love your earthly job this becomes a normal trait for everyone. But not for us in spirit bodies for all that is changed.

There are no clocks and no time clocks in heaven.

We will work but not be required to work. We will work but not be expected to work. We will work but not for money, as there is no money in heaven. We will work for love, to love and to be loved.

Look as you might you will never find a Walmart in heaven, Thank You Jesus.

You will work only when you feel like working, you will be loved for your work. Your work will be a labor of love and not for material gain. Our work will be a work of joy and love

You will be loved and appreciated for what you do out of love, for love and by love. And you will be loved for what you do out of love.

But what is key here is you will not call it work or even look at it as work. As your work will be a work of love. It will be something you want and love to do, something fulfilling and meaningful.

I have often prayed: Lord I will do any job in heaven and do it with a smile on my face and a song in my heart as long as I can be serving you in heaven. I would wash dishes, pots and pans just to be at the Banquet of the Feast of the Lamb'.

But there will be no pots and pans to wash in heaven, there will be no menial thankless jobs in heaven.

Every job will be fulfilling and every job will be a labor of love and you will be loved for doing work in heaven.

There are no bosses looking over your shoulder to watch what you do and correct you if you make a mistake.

I am not sure how it all works but you work only when you feel like working, and you do not work when you do not feel like working. There are no scheduled or time tables in heaven.

Chapter 16
HEAVEN IS OUTSIDE TIME AND SPACE

Heaven is a unique place and time. As nowhere else is like heaven. Heaven exists outside of time and space.

God has prepared this place just for us.   He loves us that much.

Our time, hours, days, weeks and years has no meaning or constraint to God.

Distance, miles, kilometers, light years etc. has no meaning or constraint to God.

2 Peter 3: 8
But beloved, be not ignorant of this one thing, that one day with the Lord is a thousand years, and a thousand years as one day.

I was once reminded to never put God in a box, no matter how big the box. I spoke once of the Universe being 146 Billion light years wide and 13.7 Billion years old (so say scientist) –

Let me be clear here I am NOT saying God made the Universe with the Big Bang 13.7 Billion years ago).   What I am saying is that – He could have, after all God is sovereign.   God is God and God will do all his pleasure.

The power of God is limitless, timeless, unfathomable and unimaginable.

Isaiah 46: 9 – 10
9 Remember the former things of old: for I am God, and there is none else; I am God, and there is none like me.

10 Declaring the end from the beginning, and from ancient times the things that are not yet done, saying, My counsel shall stand, and I will do all my pleasure.

Remember there are only two things God cannot do:
God can not lie and God cannot fail.

So, God works in mysterious ways.   God is so far above us, our tiny
3-pound human brain cannot contain the thoughts and mind of God.

God made us in his image, he loves us so much he sent his only begotten
Son to walk this earth.   To die and shed his blood for our sins.   As a way
that we could be redeemed again to enter heaven.

There is no time in heaven, no clocks, no watches.   No one cares what time
it is.   A day with our Lord can be as a thousand years and maybe even a
million or a billion years.   (Who truly knows on this earth?)

When time is meaningless what does it matter?   When you are in heaven
you will be there forever and ever without end.   So, what does it matter
about time, and it will have no meaning to you either.

In heaven time will be outside our reality.   Along with time, space and
distance will all be meaningless to us also.   This may now seem so distant
and foreign to us now, but in heaven it will seem so normal and accepted.

Remember in heaven you will never grow old; you will never have to go through the aches and pains of growing old.

And you will never have to experience the usual ailments of getting old, like wore out knees, elbows, hips you will never experience cancer, diabetes and none of the usual aches and pains of growing old.   As you will never grow old and you will never die in heaven.

In heaven in your glorified spiritual body, you will never feel tired, never require rest, you will never feel alone, you will never feel rejected.

  Somehow you will find old friends and relatives who have gone on before you.   I do not know how they will recognize you, but they will as you and they will be young again and in a spiritual body.

You will feel love, unfathomable love.

You will feel joy, unspeakable joy.

You will feel complete and whole.

You will feel like you are finally home.

You will feel like you always belonged there.

A place you came from but somehow forgot about.

Like something was missing in your old earthly body.

Like you have been wandering in the dark but now you are in the light.

But now in your glorified spiritual body you will feel whole and complete.

What I have been shown and what I have been told about heaven do not even scratch the surface of just how magnificent, joyous and wonderful heaven will actually be.

So, with all this said about heaven, you will be astounded by heaven. There is so much to see and do in heaven. You will feel that you could spend 10 lifetimes exploring it all and still not see everything.

Every day, every hour, every minute you will discover something new wonderful and amazing all the time. Every minute of every day and at every turn there is something new and wondrous to behold.

Here in your glorified spiritual body you will feel complete, whole, that nothing is undone or left out. You will feel more perfect and alive than you have ever felt before.

When you enter the presence of Jesus you will feel even more complete and more perfect, a joy and a love without reason or bounds. Pure love that is what I call it.

This only scratch the surface in regards to the Rapture and Heaven. Remember that I was NOT shown what was secret. There is much, much more not shown than what is revealed about Heaven.

Whatever your trials and tribulations here upon this earth whatever they may be, Heaven will be so much worth whatever price you pay here. Remember here is fleeting, a mist and a vapor and it's gone but Heaven will be eternal, without end and every day it will be brand new, it will never grow old and never will you.

What you will have in Heaven is joy unspeakable, love UN-measurable a peace UN-imaginable. But better than all that you will be in the presence of Jesus, the Holy Spirit and the Father and nothing could be better than that.

Several months ago, the Lord led me to write this book about my Rapture experience.

I give all praise, all glory and all honor to God.

I seek nothing for myself and all proceeds from this book will all go to my church or to further my ministry that the Lord has put in my heart..

Our time is short and as the world grows dark, we must let our light shine all the brighter,
FOR THE KING IS COMING (and soon).

God Bless you, God Keep you, and God make his face shine upon you and give you peace.

If you are not saved by the blood of Jesus, then you need to repent of you sins and get in the saving grace of Jesus Christ, Lord and Savior.

Read your King James Bible, find a true old fashion full Bible believing and teaching church. You need to join that church and humble yourself before God and pray to be in God's will and Grace and to always be pleasing to God.

You ask me is it worth it? My answer is a million times YES. Jesus paid the price for your sin and mine with his own blood. And all we have to do to be saved from HELL is to repent of our sin. Ask for forgiveness of our sin. Seek his face, truth and light by reading the Bible and heeding what it says.

Chapter 17
ADDENDUM

MY SECOND AND VERY IMPORTANT RAPTURE DREAM
My Rapture Dream of Aug. 5, 2020
I had a second Rapture dream on Aug. 5, 2020 and this was my second and a very important Rapture dream.

The dream started out with me sitting in a tall chair in a small clearing in the middle of the woods all alone. This for some strange reason did not seem odd to me it felt natural and normal for me to be sitting in this chair in the middle of the woods all alone.

All of a sudden, the Holy Spirit told me to pray. So, I closed my eyes and put my hands together before me, I bowed my head and I started praying. It seemed as though I was only about 30 seconds into my prayer when all of a sudden.

I felt just like I had been shot out of a cannon, I went straight up, up and up and up and I went faster and faster until I felt like I was moving thousands of miles per hour and then I went even faster, I felt as if I were moving faster than light.

When this first happened to me I actually gasped for air but immediately after that initial gasp for air I felt at peace, comfortable, like nothing could hurt me and it even started feeling normal in a strange kind of way. I had no idea of how long I was traveling up and up, I never opened my eyes and time escaped me as I had no concept of time any longer, time had no meaning for me any longer.

Then I became aware I was not traveling any longer, but I was standing and I heard other people around me talking. I slowly opened my eyes expecting that my eyes would have to adjust to the light in the room.

But that was not the case, when I opened my eyes, I noticed I was in this huge room more like a giant hall with many other people standing. These people were all talking amongst themselves. What I noticed was all the people in the room seemed to be in their 20s. Everyone seemed to be young, including myself. We were all dressed in brilliant white robes.

I started feeling a very real excitement. welling up inside me and I started asking the people near me very excitedly:
'DID I JUST GET RAPTURED?
DID I JUST GET RAPTURED?
I KNOW I WAS JUST RAPTURED;
I HAVE BEEN RAPTURED BEFORE AND IT FELT JUST LIKE THIS'

WAS I JUST RAPTURED?'

But for some strange reason everyone seemed busy and no one answered me.   I looked around the room (it was more like a great hall) and I noticed it was apparent the room was carved out of a solid piece of stone.

I have to explain that at this point I was so very excited. I was like a kid in a candy store (with the owner gone).   I had the biggest smile on my face and someone commented that my smile went from ear to ear.

The walls were several feet thick.   There was a staircase that went up and went outside and it was all carved out of A SOILD piece of stone.

I finally felt at peace, comfortable and finally at home. A place where I was loved beyond reason or understanding where love has no words to describe it and I felt a joy, indescribable joy and love. The cares and the worries of this earth simple melted away into nothing.   And if you were on your death bed back on this earth, that had no meaning in this place.

Then the people started talking about going into the courtyard to see Jesus and then everyone got very excited to finally see Jesus and we all began moving up the hand carved staircase into the courtyard.

But as I began to move up the staircase I woke up.
Home a place you know, a place you belong, a place where you can find peace, rest, joy and love. Home a place where you came from and a place you are returning too. A Place Called Home!

IF I keep having these Rapture dreams one day I will get Raptured for real, at least it will not be a new experience for me.

I keep getting Raptured, one day I will get to stay in heaven.

If you have ever been Raptured like I was Raptured you will spend the rest of your life trying to get back to THAT STATE of PURE LOVE, PEACE, GRACE and REST, safe and secure.

*** IMPORTANT: There are a couple of things the Holy Spirit pointed out to me in my dream.   First of all I have sever left knee pain as I have had two total knee replacement surgeries on my left knee and both of them turned out bad.

I cannot walk or stand more than about 5 to 7 minutes and then I have to sit down somewhere. SO, for me to be SITTING in a chair (before I was Raptured) seemed totally normal to me and even expected.   BUT after I was Raptured I was young again in my mid 20s and then I had no more knee pain or problems.   So then to be in a room standing seemed totally realistic and normal to me also.

***   THE SECOND POINT AND THIS IS VERY IMPORTANT: When I was asked by the Holy Spirit to pray, I only prayed about 30 seconds before I was Raptured, and I shot straight up.   So, do we ONLY have 30 seconds before the Rapture?   (30 seconds in God's time???) But remember I estimated the time from 20 seconds to 30 seconds.

YES we are that close, and YES we may only have 30 seconds IN GOD'S TIME.   I know at this point you will be asking, WHAT IS 30 SECONDS IN GOD'S TIME?   I have no idea, BUT if a thousand years can be as a day and a day can be as a thousand years, that should tell you that WE ARE VERY, VERY CLOSE.

Probably only weeks away from being Raptured out of here. (NO WE DO NOT HAVE YEARS, AS THOSE DAYS ARE LONG GONE, WE HAVE ONLY WEEKS A FEW MONTHS AT THE MOST.

My Brother Brian in Christ Jesus, is an engineer, I posed the question to him as to how much time do, we have before the Rapture. Buy his calculation we have 4 months. I do not believe that from my command to pray until I was Raptured was to set a date but only to show us that we are in the season and that time is very short.

But then you must ask yourself according to Dana Coverstone's dreams where the Holy Spirit asked the church to start praying and fasting on Sept. 1st is that the call to prayer and do, we have only 30 seconds from then?

REMEMBER, we are ONLY talking days here not months and not years. What ever we have put your time left upon this earth in the service of almighty God. As no name in heaven or on earth can save you, me or anyone from what is to come.

Judgment comes against America and it comes right quick. And this is why I am reminded of this passage in the Bible:

Matthew 24:22 AND EXCEPT THOSE DAYS SHOULD BE SHORTENED, THERE SHOULD NO FLESH BE SAVED: BUT FOR THE ELECT'S SAKE THOSE DAYS SHALL BE SHORTENED.

NOTE:

Did you know that in heaven you depend on God for everything, EVERYTHING.

Your light comes from God.

Your warmth comes from God.

The atmosphere you move through in heaven comes from God.

But you do not need air to breath as you are a spiritual being in heaven.

Your shelter comes from God.

Your sustenance comes from God (although you no longer need food, God provides you food.

In heaven you depend on God for everything.

It seems most people here depend on God for NOTHING, How Do you think that makes God feel?

You work for money, which buys your food, shelter, almost everything here.   When you get sick do you pray to God first or do you run to see your doctor first?

That is not to say that God would not use your doctor to heal you after all, ALL healing comes from God

Who do you put your faith in, the dollars in your pocket?   Or God?

Who do you look toward to supply your needs, WALMART? Or God?

I guess God will have to take our money away from us to teach us a lesson in faith.

God will take away Walmart as well.

Oh, sure when the doctors tell you that all hope is gone and you have only a few months to live THEN you get serious about God then and God is faithful and true and He will hear your sincere prayers all the time.

BUT only then do you get very serious about God, ONLY then do you put everything in God's hands ONLY at the end do you see how you should have lived all along.

And how many of these death bed prayers have been answered only to have the person turn back to their old ways, not all, but a LOT have.

God is about to give us a lesson in 'FAITH'.

We will learn to depend on God for everything.

Who knows what is best for you?   You or God?

This is not a condemnation of the faithful BUT this is a warning in love to the fence setters and those who follow false god's like money.

Oh Lord Please, is my prayer, PLEASE, PLEASE, PLEASE COME LORD JESUS

God Bless You

Watchman Tony Lamb

'HAVE BIBLE WILL TRAVEL'
A NEW CHRISTIAN GRASS ROOTS MOVEMENT

Because Today was Just Like Yesterday
Does Not Mean That Tomorrow
Will be Just Like Today

The Holy Spirit woke me a couple nights ago and told me to do this. Because of the push of satanic forces against Jesus Christ. I was told to start a push back against the darkness. I was told that a single candle shines bright in darkness.

I am not asking you to carry your Bible, BUT all I am asking you to do is to pray on this and to be led by the Holy Spirit.   The Holy Spirit asked me to carry my Bible in public everywhere I go for everyone to see. I was told that: 'If you deny Jesus before men, Jesus will deny you to the Father'. I was also told to say the Blessing over every meal that I eat.

When you cannot speak your actions and your Bible should speak for you.

Mark 8: 38
Whosoever therefore shall be ashamed of me and of my words in this adulterous and sinful generation:
of him also shall the Son of Man be ashamed, when he cometh in the glory of his Father with the holy angels.

This movement will have NO Leaders (except Jesus), NO application, NO fees all you have to do is be a believer in Jesus Christ that he died for your sins and arose on the third day and will return soon for his faithful to Rapture us out of here.

If you are Born Again and Washed in the Blood: 'It's Time To Pick Up Your Cross   (in this case your Bible) And Follow Jesus'.

Calif. is or was trying to pass a law to ban the Bible and military Christian Chaplains were banned from carrying the Bible or quoting scripture on bases.

The Holy Spirit told me it's time to PUSH BACK against the darkness.
I do what God tells me to do.

You have heard the term 'Open Carry'?

We (the Faithful in Jesus Christ) 'Open Carry' our Bibles for the world to see.

The Lord says it's time to push back against the darkness.
Together we ALL can bring light back into the world.

I now 'Open Carry' my Bible everywhere I go, how about you?
See my video on this here:
https://www.youtube.com/watch?v=V6gVmB3Q_mg

('COPY OF A LETTER I AM MAILING OUT TO ALL CHRISTIAN CHURCHES IN AMERICA')

Watchman Tony Lamb   The same God who judged
P.O. Box 41   **Israel will now judge America**
Dardanelle, AR 72834   **Judgment Comes!**

email: watchmensreport@gmail.com

youtube [Tony Lamb](over 800,000 views)
facebook [Tony Lamb]
website: www.TonyLamb.org   (Over 1 million views)

Mark 8: 38
**Whosoever therefore shall be ashamed   of me and of my words in this
adulterous and sinful generation: of him also shall the Son of
Man be ashamed, when he cometh in the glory of his Father with the holy
angels.**

Dear Fellow servant in Jesus Christ   The only thing special about me is, I am forgiven

I am just an old broken-down disabled Vietnam era Veteran who was called to be an End of Days Watchman.   I was given a multitude of dreams and visions and much more.

I am saved and I am washed in the blood. The Holy Spirit commanded me to 'WAKE UP AND TELL THE PEOPLE', I offer to speak anywhere, any place and almost any venue for free. I have spoken in several churches, I have spoken on the radio, internet, youtube and Facebook.

I was at a local, popular restaurant recently and I saw something that not only shocked me but saddened me almost to tears.   It reminded me of, the question: **'Why was Jeremiah called the weeping prophet'**?   (**He wept over what was lost**).

I too have wept over what was lost in America. I remember a time when in America television stations all closed down at midnight or sooner with a closing prayer.   I also remember a time when pastors carried A KJV Bible everywhere they went, & not a cell phone and I also remember when all Christians said the blessing over every meal.

What I saw in that restaurant were three preachers from local churches in the restaurant. The sad thing was that not one of them had a Bible with them.   I also saw several deacons from local churches and none of them had a Bible either. But the really sad thing was that   NOT ONE PERSON in the restaurant said the blessing over their meal.

Except for me, I had my KJV Bible on the table and I said the blessing and I did not care who saw me or who heard me. (We are commanded to be a peculiar people unto Jesus Christ).

The Holy Spirit asked me to pick up my Bible and follow Jesus.   I now carry my KJV Bible everywhere I go. I am asking you & your church to join me. Be led by the Holy Spirit pick up your cross, (your KJV Bible) and follow Jesus & '**Say The Blessing Over Every Meal**'.
The Holy Spirit told me it was important now more than ever in these last days to let our light shine, (A SINGLE CANDLE shines bright in the dark).   After all, consider what Jesus did and suffer for you and me, it's a small thing but means so much these Last Days!

I was asked to carry my KJV Bible everywhere I go, Walmart shopping, doctor's offices, dentist office, eating out, everywhere and to (SAY THE BLESSING over every meal).
One Day It Will Be Illegal to Carry a Bible, Say the Blessing or even Pray in Public.
                        (WILL YOU STAND UP FOR JESUS THEN?) - ((OR NOW?))

I CARRY MY KJV BIBLE EVERYWHERE I GO (AND YOU SHOULD TOO).
If you see me without my Bible it's because I have given my Bible away.
Consider this; **If you deny Jesus to men then Jesus will deny you to the Father**.
Have you heard that before?   It's time to let your light shine and not hide it under a bushel basket.   **(Why take a chance?)**

We would occasionally eat at a popular Mexican restaurant that serves alcoholic drinks (I DO NOT DRINK) but I would place my Bible on the table in that place and say the blessing over the meal.

When you cannot speak let your actions and your KJV Bible show, declare, and speak for you that YOU are a Christian and that you are not denying Jesus (and never will).

Please pray on this and join me in this Last Days Crusade?   If you feel uncomfortable using my name to promote this, then (promote it as your own idea) as it is the message here that is important (and NOT ME).   There are NO fees to join, NO applications to fill out, NO executives (except for Jesus) and NO leaders except for the (Holy Spirit).
                * PLEASE PRAY ON THIS AND BE LEAD BY THE HOLY SPIRIT IN THIS *

Remember if you get Raptured out of Walmart shopping your KJV Bible will be left behind as your only testament that you are a Christian and you have just been Raptured. And if they are left behind staring at your Bible then they should know that they are in a lot of trouble.

You can rubber stamp church info on the inside covers and pass these Bibles out at Hospital waiting rooms, doctor offices, dentist offices, even auto repair shop waiting rooms or even pass these Bibles out door to door to anyone needing a Bible.   You can give FREE Bibles to visitors at your church.   What God needs in these last days is Hell Fire & Brimstone, ON FIRE Pastors.

IN THESE LAST DAYS GOD NEEDS 'ON FIRE' PASTORS?   TIME IS SHORT!

God Is Calling YOU to become; ON FIRE FOR JESUS, and preach the full gospel.

GOD IS ABOUT TO MOVE A HEAVY HAND AGAINST AMERICA.

You can buy BIG KJV Bibles cheap in bulk 24 to a case for $1.24 each (includes shipping) from: Bibles in Bulk, POB 3477 Peabody, MA 01961 ph. 800-944-6360   website: www.biblesinbulk.com   ***((I have no affiliation with this company))***
Visit my website for more details at: **www.TonyLamb.org**
(ECONOMIC COLLAPSE IS COMING)

God Bless You
Tony Lamb
ADDENDUM   From the desk of Tony Lamb   (**www.TonyLamb.org**)

I do not claim to be a Prophet.   But my dreams and Visions and contact I have had with the Holy Spirit have given me unique insight into what is coming.

The Holy Spirit came to me about 4 years ago and hovered above me in my bed. I never opened my eyes but I felt His presence above me so close I felt I could reach up and touch Him.   Then the Holy Spirit spoke in an audible voice that I heard with my own ears and He told me that:
'AMERICA IS ENTERING JUDGMENT'.

Then about 3 years ago the Holy Spirit came to me in the same manor and spoke to me in an audible voice and this time He said: 'AMERICA IS ENTERING THE TIME OF SORROWS'.

And then 2 years ago the Holy Spirit came to me in the same manor and told me that: 'AMERICA IS BABYLON AND AMERICA WOULD BE DESTROYED IN ONE HOUR'. Then the Holy Spirit told me to read (Jeremiah 51 and Revelation 18) and He said it was; 'IMPORTANT'.   Maybe you should read it also?

My dreams and visions have given me glimpses into what is coming.
WE ARE IN THE TIME OF SORROWS NOW (The Birth Pangs) of the Bible.
And 'things' are ONLY going to get worse, and then worse and worse. And sometime before the Tribulation starts the Rapture of the faithful will occur.   God's Master Plan is in motion and no amount of praying and fasting at this point can stop or change what is coming.

Sin will continue to abound unabated. The price of food will continue to rise, famine is coming to America. Power will become hit and miss and as time goes on it will become more miss than hit. Eventually the power will go out.

The world economy will collapse and it will hit America especially hard. It will seem as if everyone is out of work.   Revolution and War will be coming to America and soon.

There will be massive earthquakes, Tsunami's, volcanoes, and even two asteroid strikes. One in the Atlantic and another over Western Canada. These will wreck ecological havoc on the world.   War is coming to America and I saw foreign troops on American soil, I saw atomic bombs going off in major American cities. I saw an EMP strike shut down all electricity in America. This Corona virus is sweeping our nation and our economy will not survive and America will be hit very hard and a depression deeper than 1929 is coming.   (But the faithful will be Raptured out of here at some point and VERY SOON!)

TIME IS SHORT!   -   BEFORE ONE WOE ENDS ANOTHER WOE BEGINS

America has sinned a great sin and:
THE SAME GOD WHO JUDGED ISRAEL HARSHLY WILL NOW JUDGE AMERICA EVEN MORE HARSH!

WHAT WE SAY AND WHAT WE DO NOW IN THESE LAST HOURS AND LAST MINUTES IS MORE IMPORTANT THAN YOU COULD EVER IMAGINE.

*My new audio CD is included and is available on the website and a copy has been mailed to your local Christian Talk Radio Station, So PLEASE call your favorite local station and ask them to play THE WARNING by Tony Lamb

*Calling all born again Christians to humble yourself and be in prayer at 8 PM CST (adjust your time accordingly) so we are all in prayer all over America at the same time. Pray for our leaders, military, our states, Police, first responders, fire department, doctors, nurses everyone who has lost because of this virus and for those about to lose everything. Pray for Repentance, Renewal, Rededication & Revival, pray for Acts 2:17 Pray as Nineveh Prayed in sackcloth and ashes. Desperate times call for desperate measures, Pray as if it's your last day on earth.
  (WE WILL ALL BE FASTING AND IN PRAYER THIS SEPT & NOVEMBER, SOMETHING BIG IS COMING)

(God Bless you & keep you & yours)   **(I was called for this time right now, to WARN THE PEOPLE, TO WARN YOU)**
I AM JUST THE DUST OF THE EARTH – BUT I AM GOD'S DIRT!
Watchman Tony Lamb
www.TonyLamb.org

As God comes to the wicked as an avenger, he comes to the righteous as a redeemer.   Isaiah the prophet wrote 26:12 "The Lord is going to keep you in perfect peace – if you'll simply trust him".

The Lord says I haven't given you a spirit of fear but of power, love and sound mind. 2 Timothy 1:7.

Even in the most difficult of times we will enjoy great blessing because God will reveal himself as never before.

This book is dedicated to:
Daniel,
Brian,
Crystal,
Zachary,
Paige,
Joshua,
Mason,
Mariah,
Sydney,

Rylee,
Tyler,
Tim,
Terry,
Sarah,
Erin,
Tim Jr.,
John,
Diana
and many others unnamed. I love you and miss you terribly. I pray God keep you and make his face shine upon you and give you peace!

See my new web site, I have tons of FREE stuff at: www.tonylamb.org

(I am not a Minister, Deacon or even a Sunday School Teacher)
But I am a born again, washed in the blood of Jesus,
Watchman with dreams and visions for the soon return of Jesus Christ.

If you would like to contact me in regards to giving my testimony at your church or function (I do not charge a fee for speaking) email me at: watchmensreport(at)gmail.(com)

My physical address is: Tony Lamb,   P.O. Box 41, Dardanelle, AR 72834

If you would like to see my many videos go to www.youtube.com and in the [search] box type in Tony Lamb and it should take you to my youtube channel page. Thank You

My other books include:
'GOD SHOWED ME THE FUTURE – America Is Entering Judgement'
by Tony Lamb

'MY DREAMS AND VISIONS – And Contact I Have Had With The Holy Spirit'
by Tony Lamb

'IF THE RAPTURE DON'T COME SOON – There Should Be No Flesh Left To Save'
by Tony Lamb

WHAT HAPPENS WHEN YOU TELL GOD 'NO' – I Am Just The Dust Of The Earth – But I Am God's Dirt'
By Tony Lamb

If you would like additional copies of this or any of my books go to www.amazon.com

Or you can find a list of all my books on my web site at:
www.TonyLamb.org

Thank You

God Bless You

Tony Lamb

A humble Watchman and Servant

Of the Most High God

Who sits upon the Throne

Above All.

In Jesus name I pray.

AMEN

Made in USA - Kendallville, IN
20087_9781695677159
12.06.2021 1727